The Bakery

– JEFF BEACH –

To Stuart

Have a good read

FASTPRINT PUBLISHING
PETERBOROUGH, ENGLAND

Jeff

THE BAKERY
Copyright © Jeff Beach 2009

ISBN 978-184426-674-6

First published 2009 by
FASTPRINT PUBLISHING
Peterborough, England.

Printed by
www.printondemand-worldwide.com

DEDICATION

I would like to dedicate this book to Millie (my Dusky) who, though I could not put a word to it, I loved with an all-consuming and everlasting passion, and somehow managed to let down so very badly, and who I couldn't, and wouldn't forget.

Also to Hazel, a very special lady who, through her own unselfish love, had the courage to tackle an ageing bachelor who had told her repeatedly there could never be another woman. And finally taught me, first to live again, and eventually, in spite of all my doubts, to love again, and so gave me forty-two years of total fulfilment, that I really didn't deserve, and left a void that can never be filled.

And because of a strange anomaly with the initials, to any woman anywhere who shared their initials of MH or MM, particularly if she had black, or at least dark, shoulder-length hair.

Finally, I would like to dedicate this book to the real stars. The men and the women who, through their ambition and foresight, caused four hundred square yards of common land to be fenced off, a pile of bricks and a goat to be put on that land, and the bakery to be built and to prosper, by and large, for almost two hundred years. Based on the people whose stories, given all the facts that I could assimilate, I have tried as faithfully as possible to tell.

JEFF BEACH

The Bakery
By Jeff Beach

There is no reason to mention John Barlow in this narrative. He never knew anything about the bakery, but without him the place wouldn't have been built, and this story couldn't have been penned. And anyway, his story should be known.

John Barlow was born in the year 1800, so these events must have happened around 1806/7. This is his story, told in his own words, even though he must have been illiterate. Most people were in the year of his birth. But John was a learned man, only his knowledge was more of the earth, a self-educated man of the world, as it were. Only he wasn't a man, he was just a boy.

He knew which tree was pliable, and so could be fashioned into a bed or a fishing net, how to fasten the wood and give it time to accustom itself to its strange shape and so not break. He knew which tree gave the most heat so that they were never cold, and then how to dampen the flames so that they wouldn't all roast in their beds. And he could build a house stable enough to have no fear of whatever inclement weather might be levelled against them.

He knew the names of every tree in the woods, how to travel through them in the worst of winter's wrath. The way to catch enough food so they never went hungry, of how to set his traps, and the trails of all the meat in the woods, so that his father wasn't needed any more. If only he could make Sara understand.

But then Sara would learn all he knew, and some things he could never know, and then he would be afraid that, just as he didn't need father, Sara didn't need him.

But I overrun myself...

John's Story (Chapter One)

My earliest recollection was being made to stand with my sister Sara and the three younger kids and watch my grossly misshapen, naked, screaming and cursing mother, writhing in agony on the hard-dry dusty clay floor of our little cott. It was as if I had been born at that moment. I could remember nothing before then, and everything afterwards.

It was just the way that father was, he decided we all had to watch mother rolling in her own slime, to witness all the blasphemies and we dare not move. After that day I had no more fear of my father, no more respect, nothing.

Sara was eventually sent to fetch the wise woman, who seemed to take an eternity to arrive.

The wise woman, a mixture of midwife, soothsayer, holy woman, and more than half way to being a witch, immediately took charge as she saw what was happening. We saw the hard look of anger on her face, the calm, piercing eyes as she looked first at mother, then she turned to face father, her black, penetrating eyes seeming to make him shrink before her. Only then concentrating her attention on the twisted, writhing distended body, which now seemed to have slime oozing from every orifice. Her cursing and screaming had now subsided to a sort of gurgling rattle, as though she hadn't the strength to make a louder noise. I can still see father's helpless, pathetic face.

I had seldom seen father cowed by anyone, let alone a woman, but this woman seemed to look right through him with an intensity of hate.

She turned to us kids.

"Outside." Then, she spoke to father. "I hope you are proud of yourself. Did you want your kids to see how you have killed their mother?"

Her voice was loud enough to carry through the wattle and daub walls, so that we heard her continuing, "Get me some hot water so I can clean the mess up, and then get outside with your kids."

We had a log fire built in the centre of the room, and a hole so that the smoke was drawn up through the roof, which kept the winter's cold at bay. Our cott was just a normal wattle and daub shelter, originally just one of the one-sided structures that were scattered across the moors and scrublands that stretched away towards the sunset, and then north as far as the desolate peak district, and the Pennine hills that were miles farther to the north. This was a wild, lawless area that we kids knew only from hearsay, but we knew enough not to venture any farther than the immediate vicinity. Many an unwary traveller had vanished into the bogs that were scattered throughout the common lands.

We had heard the tales of others who had been robbed by the highwaymen and footpads, who alone seemed to have knowledge of the wastes.

The cotts were scattered throughout the common lands since time immemorial, and had been built originally to shelter the shepherds and their flocks in the harsh winter weather. Many a life of man or animal had been saved by the cotts.

Father joined us outside after a while, his face stark and white, looking as if he had just been to the fires of hell, and the ultimate damnation, and had not liked to contemplate their fury.

All us kids sat together on a grass tussock. Father was a little further away on a log, but well within earshot, in case he was called. His face hung down, his back was bent, he looked as if he had aged and for the first time he seemed to me like an old man. He just sat there as though he wished the very earth would swallow him up.

"Come here." We had sat there a long time in complete silence when the woman's voice eventually came from the doorway. "I hope you can forgive yourself because God never will."

Father muttered something unintelligible.

The wise woman's voice was commanding, "Send the kids away somewhere, and make sure they don't come back in a hurry."

When father eventually spoke his voice was crackly, uncertain.

"I didn't know, she had always been all right before, I thought the kids had a right to see what happened."

"Get rid of them."

I thought father would argue but he came out.

"Sara and John, take the sleigh and the axe and go through the woods and chop some logs for the fire."

The sleigh consisted of two poles, with some willow lashed to hold them together. We often used it to bring some wood for the cold nights.

The woman said, "Don't come back till it starts to go dark."

I noticed Sara was trembling. She whispered as we walked along the track, although we were too far away to be heard now, "What will became of us?"

It was almost as if I was the elder and she was the child.

"I don't know Sis, but we have to stick together."

We pulled the sleigh along, into the great forest of Sherwood which stretched for miles towards the sunrise. I held her hand, it was the first time, we usually fought like cats and dogs, but adversity makes strange bedfellows. And right then we thought it was we two against the world, and in a way it was.

Summer had already passed, but today had been warm, the type of day father always called an 'Indian summer', whatever that might mean.

We chopped down a little sapling birch tree and then cut it into logs. They were neatly stacked and securely tied with some willow cord onto the sleigh. It is surprising how concentrating on heavy manual work temporarily dulls the mind to life's problems. Of course, as we trudged home along familiar paths, with the sun already dipping low over the trees, and darkness beginning to envelope us, our unspoken fear became more and more real.

Normally, we would have had to hurry back as quickly as we could, and usually had a clout for loitering. Today we made the task last as long as we could, fearful of what would happen when we got home.

The fading sun was already casting long shadows behind the trees and the inevitable chill of the cloudless autumnal sky, and the future's uncertainty, was starting to make us tremble as we entered the small clearing that surrounded our cott.

The young kids were gone, we knew not where, and we never saw them again. The shell of what had, only yesterday, been a strong, self-reliant man now seemed hesitant, unsure of himself, almost more childlike than we were.

There was no trace of the earlier drama. Fresh reeds had been cut and now lay on the floor, a job that had always been done by mother. There was a damp patch, which had been covered by a thicker layer of reeds but nonetheless was still visible, and rather more flies seemed attracted to the spot.

We had already stacked the logs and, because we had no orders to do anything else, I said to Sis, "We had better go to bed."

At the same time I looked towards father half expecting to be told to do something. He remained silent.

The bed consisted of two birch poles as the outer edge and several thinner ones running parallel. Willow trigs had been interwoven between them to lash the whole lot together and it made a sturdy structure. At the side where our heads lay, it had been lashed round another thick piece of birch so that we were lifted off the floor, and a thick layer of reeds lay across the frame making us comfortable enough.

The whole seven of us had slept together, mum, father and us five kids. We were usually warm enough, even in the coldest winter night, but if we weren't, there was always the cover, which was made of some sort of animal skins, that could be used at a last resort. Now, with just Sara and me it seemed a huge space. Father just sat outside, neither of us had the temerity to ask him to join us. From long experience we knew better than question anything that he did.

It was the first time in my life that I ever lay awake the whole of the night, and I'm sure Sara didn't close her eyes either.

The following morning, after looking towards father to see if he had snapped out of his lethargy, and seeing nothing to indicate there was any change in his mood, I went out on the edge of the woods and set some snares, for either rabbits or anything else that stumbled into them. The weather that had for so long been so very pleasant had taken a decided turn for the worse. There was a cutting wind lashed with rain, and it was definitely colder. We were on the south facing edge of a ridge that ran east to west. Pleasant enough when the weather was good, but winds always swirled themselves through the gully, and at these times we got the very worst of the weather.

At the bottom of the slope there was a little stream, which supplied us with clear water, and in the woods were enough berries to supply our needs. We kept ourselves clear of people as much as we could, but when I saw some men marking out the ground around the stream, I was curious, and at the same time concerned. What could they be doing? I knew that for weeks they had been digging a great trench that stretched far away across the commons and out towards the setting sun.

Once I dared to ask father what it was and he replied, "Nothing to do with us, keep away from them."

But now they were measuring in our stream, pegs had been driven into the ground on either bank; it looked as if they were going to dig their ditch straight through our water supply. Even I could see that would be a calamity, what could we drink then?

Of course, even in our short lifetime, we had seen more and more people around, but normally we just avoided them.

I remembered father once going to the market in Alfreton town. He took some rabbits and came back with second-hand clothes for himself and mother. Sara even got some of mother's things. We thought we were rich. He even got the axe that we used for chopping down trees. It was in a very rusty state but father rubbed it on a stone and made it sharp. Then with constant use it got to be pretty good.

I remember mother saying, "All this for a few rabbits?"

Father replied, "It's a case of knowing when to take them. If a man is hungry he'll give anything to feed his family."

I knew of the great lord who lived in a castle of Codnor, about two miles away. I knew about the pits and the men who crawled in the bowels of the earth to get coal and iron ore. I'd seen them walking by, like zombies, their faces black as any man from the jungle that I'd seen in a picture book once. I'd even seen with my own eyes the great forge, less than a mile away, that seemed like hell's own inferno as it belched out flames into the night sky.

They called this place Derbyshire, and it was the centre of the whole world.

The following day, which was my seventh birthday, I got my rabbit. Sarah skinned and gutted it, and she collected some herbs for the flavour. We would all feed well for the next couple of days.

Nothing would be wasted. The meat was for now. The bones would make a nice stew after they had boiled in water for twenty-four hours.

I even collected some berries to make it into a real feast. Autumn was the time of plenty for berries.

The skin would be scraped and cleaned and when joined together with others would eventually make a rug, or even a cloak, like the one father wore in the cold and snows of winter.

I'd never known father go out to do any paid work, but we all lived like lords, and it wasn't very often we felt hungry.

I said to Sara, "It doesn't really matter about father, now that I'm seven, I'll be able to catch enough for us now."

I don't remember if she replied.

I'd been out early in the morning, checked and reset the snares, and was hungry as I returned, or maybe it was the smell of the cooking rabbit. Sara had put out a portion for the three of us. I looked towards father.

"Does he want any?" I asked.

"He has to eat," was her reply.

We had plates made of tin, but they served their purpose well enough.

Father was still sitting on the log, much the same spot as he occupied for the last day and a half. Now, as if the smell had stirred some forgotten sense, he moved his head in our direction.

It was Sara who spoke; I don't think I could have brought myself to utter a word.

"We've got some rabbit, come and get some."

He looked towards us for some time, as though uncomprehending, or maybe it was being told to fetch it (mother would always have run to take it to him), before finally getting up somewhat shakily and coming to collect it.

In the next few weeks life continued in this new pattern. I caught enough to feed us all, rabbits, hedgehogs, a fox, anything that strayed into the traps. Berries were plentiful, but both Sara and I knew that the coming winter would be the big test.

In the meantime the great ditch snaked past us and joined onto another coming from the other way. In no time it was full of water and strange craft appeared on it.

I knew of a spring in the woods so we could fetch some water when we wanted it. It wasn't so convenient but we would manage all right.

I even went down to the canal and talked to the bargemen. If I stood on the bank I could talk to them without being in any danger of them grabbing me. But they didn't seem to mean me any harm. There was a problem in understanding what they said, it seemed to be English, but it was strange somehow.

I found out they were transporting coal, all the way to a big river in the south called the Trent, and then over some more canals to a huge place known as London. This place was bigger than Alfreton.

There were coal pits and iron ore mines all over the moors, and on waste scrublands. There always had been, but there seemed to be more and more now. They were even starting to build a whole new village on the other side of what had been the stream, and was now the canal. This had been no more than scrublands. I was told this would be called Ironville so that people who dug out the iron-ore, or worked at the great smelting forges, would have a place to live. But where would all these people come from? It just didn't make sense. There couldn't be so many people in the whole world.

One thing was becoming more and more certain. There wouldn't be any room to live in the little cotts for much longer. It was less than half a mile down to the valley. It was strange that we hadn't been spotted already, but the people who had dug out the great ditch had been so busy they seemed to just dig and dig and now the thing was full of water. No sooner was it finished than the great barges began taking coal away, not just one, but lots of them. This was a whole new world.

I tried to speak to father, though it was abhorrent to do so. Somehow he had to wake up to the fact that everything that we knew was going to end.

"It's not going to be long before they want to chop all the trees down and build something here, then what shall we do? Without the rabbits we will starve."

"We will go further into the woods," the old man replied. It was the first thing he had said since all our family had gone. But he was not really taking in the enormity of it all.

"The woods won't be big enough for them, we won't have a chance."

I tried to talk to Sara, but she didn't seem to want to know.

Instead of the horses and carts taking away the coal, it was now the barges piled high with the black stuff, and whole unwashed families, men, women and kids down to the tiniest tots, covered in coal dust, filling them up, and going away, to make room for the next barge from dawn to dusk.

The world that we knew was almost gone.

Without saying anything to the others I made my way down the twitchel, a narrow track through the woods, past a little hamlet known as Summer-cotts and deep into the trees beyond. In a place I would learn was called the Birch Woods I found a nice little cott, far enough from any houses, with a spring close by. It didn't look as if anyone had been near for years. I started to cut some saplings and with enough daub of nearby mud, it was soon four-sided and weatherproof. I was proud of my efforts. There was nothing that I couldn't do. I didn't need anyone to help me. We would be safe here, a mile or two away from where the people were spoiling all our lives.

I asked Sara to come with me to Alfreton market, we could sell the spare rabbits. Winter was coming and father always said that was the time to go, people were hungrier then and we would get more. We would be able to buy something we needed for the new house.

"We will have to ask father," she said.

I believed I was the man about the house now, while he seemed no more than an empty shell. I didn't like the idea of asking him anything. She asked him anyway. He said we couldn't go, so she wouldn't go.

"I don't care," I said, "I'm going anyway."

I went to Alfreton, it was only about three miles away. I put on father's old coat, and a belt so that I could hang about eight rabbits from it, down the inside of the coat so no one would see them and try to steal them from me. I was surprised that the coat nearly fitted me. I'd grown so much in the last couple of months, and filled out as well. I went through the Ryddings where they had cut down a whole lot of trees years ago, long before my time, and along the pathway they called the Greenhill track. Then through the Summer-cotts common, which stretched a long way from Sommer-cotts hamlet, down the scrublands following the lea moor. I saw the stream, which looked clear enough for drinking, and there were some abandoned cotts that could be made habitable. They wouldn't be any use to us though, there wasn't any tree cover and we would soon be found and thrown out. I thought of how grown-up I was to have thought of that. I kept to the highest ground through the moors, so that I wouldn't get stuck in a bog, and I was soon in Alfreton market.

I didn't like the smell of the place. Open drains ran down the middle of the hill and all the way through the market. The quicker I could get away the better. There seemed more people than I had ever seen in my life.

I swapped three rabbits for another axe. It was a rusty thing, bigger than our axe, and the handle was broken. I'd soon cut some wood to mend that, and I saw how quickly father had cleaned and sharpened the old one we had got. And I got a rug as well, or it could be used as a coat with some string to tie it together. It was made of leather.

I was making my way down the hill when I heard a man say, "There he is, what's he doing with that rug, he must have pinched it."

They were making their way towards me, and I wasn't going to stand and argue. I slipped between some of the hovels, and even had time to think they were a lot worse than my new cott, then ran a fast as I could. I slid between some taller and even more rickety buildings, joined together with stairs that seemed to belong to several different places. Planks stretched across from one upstairs building to the next, as though waiting for the next good wind to clear the lot. The stench that permeated the entire confines was probably worse to my nose, used to the great outdoors, than to those used to dwelling within this depressing place that others seemed to be able to live within. The carcases of dead rats and decaying, half-eaten dogs lay rotting in gutters running with urine, and worse, thrown from the upper windows of these flimsy dwellings. The whole lot was fortunately built on an incline, which allowed the waste to trickle down the slope. This place shouldn't have been called Alfreton. Surely it was hell itself.

Then I came out the other side of the buildings and in a clearing a man was scraping, with a blade fastened between two handles, what seemed to be an animal skin, probably a cow. The coarse, black skin peeled away and the skin seemed almost white, before he dipped it again in a vat of stinking liquids and hung it to dry. I would find out later he had been making leather. Now, however, I was in no position to ask him. I slid by him and into the shadows, back between the hovels. I didn't think he had seen me.

The two men were still following. "Have you seen a kid with a leather coat?" one asked.

"He's not come down here."

"Must have gone the other way then."

They nipped into another gap between the buildings and went out of view.

I kept quite still for a while then, eventually, he spoke.

"I don't think it will be long before they are back."

I stepped out and he saw the coat.

"Just where did you get that?" he asked, not confrontationally, but in a matter-of-fact way.

"I swapped it for some rabbits, with a woman on the market."

"I hope you aren't lying, it's one of mine."

"No, I swear it."

"I believe you, I know that pair. Get into the hut and lie on the bed, put the coat over you and wait."

I waited, the axe against my leg, my one sure hope of defence if it was a necessity. Eventually I heard some movement, which I thought was the tanner who had come into the hut. The cover was pulled roughly from me and I tightened my hand on the axe. But it was only the woman from the market.

"Thomas, he's just what he says he is, and here are the rabbits to prove it."

"I wanted to believe you lad, and I know only too well what those men are like, a bad lot to be tangling with. You say you come from where they are making the canal. They say it's a marvel to behold. They call that place the Golden Valley, because of all the money people are getting from the pits, the barges, the forges and the ironworks."

I wanted to show that I wasn't just a kid, and I knew what was happening as well, so I said, "They are going to build a whole new town for the workers, and they are calling it the Ironville, after the iron pits and the ironworks."

Thomas' mouth was actually drooling as he continued.

"There will be so much more money around, they will want new leather coats, belts and everything."

His wife joined in. "Not in our lifetime, all we will ever know is hard work."

"What does your dad do?" Thomas asked.

I was taken unawares and didn't know what to say. Eventually I replied, "Nothing, well not since mother died. He's not like he was, I have to be the man about the place now. We manage all right though."

"Where exactly do you live?"

"In one of those cotts the old shepherds used to use."

"They are only windbreaks."

"No, father did it up, put a roof on and made it cosy. It's all right now, only they took our water when they built the canal and I have to go a long way to a spring to get fresh water."

"That doesn't seem a good life."

"Oh it is, but I'm trying to get Sara to come with me to a new place that I've done up myself, and that is much nearer to the spring."

Thomas was looking at me. He only saw a seven-year-old boy as he smiled at his wife. "Is Sara your girl?"

"No, Sara is my sister."

"Somebody will probably throw you out of the cotts, and then what will you do?"

"We always lived there, no one has tried to throw us out yet."

"Will your father live with you as well?"

"I don't want him, he murdered our mother, and he made all us kids watch."

Thomas looked at his wife, then back at me. He was shocked and intrigued at the same time.

"How did he murder her… why?"

"The wise woman came, she said he murdered her."

Gradually, bit by bit, the tanner and his wife sorted out what had happened.

"The lad's had a frightful ordeal Martha."

She turned to me.

"Things like that happen sometimes, I don't think your father wanted it to happen."

"The wise woman said he did, and he made us watch."

"Some men are like that, they think children should know what happens."

"He didn't make us watch before."

"Having a baby is a big thing for a woman, but if they like their man they want to do it," the woman said.

"Martha!" Thomas spoke sharply.

Martha continued, "Thomas and me have been wanting a baby for years, but it hasn't happened."

"But everybody can have babies. We have got five, and we nearly had another, used to have anyway, why did we need any more?"

Martha turned away and Thomas went and put his arm around her.

I looked first at one, then the other. I didn't know what I had said, but something clearly had upset them both. They didn't look as if they were getting over it, so I said, "I had better go."

"No lad, you don't have to go, it's not your fault, but... " He had pulled away from his wife. "But I suppose they will be wondering where you have got to, and I have got to do a bit more work before dark."

"Thank you," I said.

"For what?"

"For hiding me from them," I indicated the way the men had gone an hour or so before, "and just talking to me."

"Yes, now we have to make sure they don't see you getting away."

"It would be better if he went up past the *George*, on to the church, and came down behind the horse-wash, on the opposite side of town. He could cut through Swanwick common and follow the canal. He would make his way back, till he found his home," Martha said.

I looked from one to the other. "I don't know these things. What is a church, and a George and a horse-wash?"

"You know a church surely, a big building where people go to pray. The *George* is the new pub at the top of the town, and the horse-wash is just a big smelly pond, down at the bottom of the hill."

I smiled. "Smelly, worse than in there?" I indicated the tannery with its vats of evil liquid.

Now Martha smiled as well. "We don't seem to notice that," she said.

Martha led me outside to the vats and then pointed to the left. "Just go to the top of the hill, you'll see a big white building, that's the *George*, go straight past it. Keep straight on, by the top of the market, and you'll come to the church. Follow the path down the other side of the houses, at the bottom of the hill is the pond, they call that the horse-wash. Keep going across the common till you find something that you know."

I must have looked unsure. "Sounds a long way."

"Only the same distance as you came to get here."

"Thank you," I said.

"Oh, and if you come back, be very careful, those men will be ready for you, and you might not see them next time."

"It's good of you Mrs."

"You can drop us in a couple of rabbits now and again." She smiled at me, and I thought what a nice person she was.

As I set out, it came to my mind that it was the first time I had said thank you since my mother used to prompt me to say it. She always used to say, "Remember your manners."

I was thinking of my mother as I began the trek back home, and as I thought it transferred to anger against his father.

I hurried past the pub but loitered at the church, looking at the inscriptions on the stones. I couldn't read them, of course, but somehow they seemed to have some significance.

Then a strangely-dressed man, with long robes, came towards me and asked if I was looking for someone.

"No," I said, somewhat startled.

"I thought you seemed to be searching for some name, some special grave."

"No," I said, backing away.

I continued down the path without looking behind me, and once round the corner, began to run down the slope behind the hovels and soon came upon the horse-wash with its flies and yes, its own peculiar smell, similar to, but not quite like the tanner's vats.

I didn't stop, but ran past the water. Then I thought I recognised something about the common land, but all common land looks about the same. I also knew enough to keep to the higher land, and make generally away from the direction of the afternoon sun. Sooner or later I was bound to see the trees, then I would know just where I was.

It was the Ryddings I saw first, so it was only down the hill to our cott.

Today had been the biggest adventure of my life. I'd proved to myself I could manage, no matter what happened.

I told Sara about Alfreton. "You should see all those people, more than we have ever seen in our life."

Sara seemed impressed with my new coat, and the axe, even with its broken handle.

"I'll soon make another handle, and next time I'll bring something for you, and for the new cott."

I told her about the tanners, and how the lady said I could bring her some more rabbits. Oh, and the terrible smell from the vats, they didn't seem to notice it though. I didn't mention about having to hide from those men. Perhaps one day Sara would go into to town. I didn't want to frighten her so that she wouldn't go.

I even told her about the man dressed in some outlandish clothes. He wore a long white robe and had a funny band round his neck. He was something to do with the church.

"What is a church?" she asked

"It's a big place, with stones sticking up all round it."

She looked dubious but didn't say anything else.

All this made me feel even more grown-up. I was a real man of the world now.

"Have you asked father about the new cott?", Sara asked, cutting into my thoughts. "He might not want to go."

I looked towards where he sat huddled, like some old man in a corner. "What good is he? We don't need him."

Sara just turned away.

The following day I went to see the new cott. I was in for a shock, it had all been pulled down. I just stood looking in sheer disbelief. The roof had been pulled off and the sides levelled. What harm could it be doing to anyone? Perhaps some farmer considered this to be his land and he didn't want anyone to intrude on his patch.

After the initial shock I thought, what did it matter, there were plenty of other places to build myself another shelter. I was just glad I hadn't put anything of value in it, like my new axe, or that would have been lost. I would just try again somewhere else.

I was carrying my new axe with its broken handle, as well as the old one, so that I could cut down a birch sapling to make the handle. I had gone some distance into the woods away from where my new cott had stood, when I found a suitable sapling and began to chop it down. As I swung the axe at it, I became angry that anyone should have smashed down such a nice hut that wasn't doing anyone any harm. The sapling soon splintered and fell down, now I became more relaxed as I shaped the handle. It fitted smugly into the base of the new axe and inwardly I congratulated myself on a job well done. All the time I was gaining experience in doing these jobs.

I walked on deeper into the woods, generally exploring the area.

Some way from the birch wood I come across three ponds, with a little stream draining the first into the second, then the third. The water looked clear enough and I thought it seemed a nice enough place, and what's more, I hadn't seen any farms nearby. But neither had I seen any cotts.

I sat down on some stones and began to sharpen the rusty blade on my new axe. It seemed to take a lot longer than when father had done the old one, but gradually it began to look good.

A man was sitting with a piece of stick and a string hanging from it into the water. I walked over to where he was and stood watching for quite a while, totally fascinated. Looking into the ponds, I saw there were fish swimming in it. I remembered father had brought a fish home once; perhaps he had been to this place. Eventually the man turned and looked up at me.

"They aren't biting today."

I looked from him and to the water, not quite comprehending how he expected to catch a fish with that.

"You haven't seen anyone fishing before, have you?"

"No."

"Look, all you do is put a hook on the end of the rope, if it's got a worm as well they try to catch it, and you have them on the hook. You need a lot of time, practice and patience."

I stood looking into the clear water, there seemed to be an awful lot of fish.

"Why don't you just grab one?"

"Easier said than done lad."

I went and stood in the water and grabbed at the fish. It wasn't long before I got hold of one, but it spun out of my hand and escaped. I gave up after a while, but I knew I could catch one with a bit of practice.

The man said, "Can you swim?"

It wasn't a term I had heard before and I didn't know what he meant.

"The water is pretty deep and a lot of people have drowned in there."

I might not really understand, but I knew enough to be careful.

I stood there for a while and it began to drizzle, but the spots accumulated on the leaves and dropped as big spots on us. The man didn't bother at all. He had a makeshift shelter partly covering him.

After a while I began to move away, I wasn't used to just idling around. Besides, I wanted to see if I had caught anything in the traps, and I needed to find somewhere to erect another shelter. There seemed to be getting more and more people around the canal, soon someone would find us and we really needed another place to go.

Chapter 2

The next day I persuaded Sara to come to see the spring. She had to know where to go if it happened to be needed. I told her what happened to the new hut. "Don't worry I'll soon find another spot," I added.

She seemed totally indifferent, as though this were of no concern to her. I was really trying to make her understand that we wouldn't be able to stay where we were for much longer and it might be better to be nearer the spring, or another one like it.

I didn't know then that things were about to take a dramatic turn.

We returned home and father had sufficiently stirred from his lethargy to be standing outside. He was staring down through the trees at the canal.

There was quite a commotion. The whole canal seemed to be on fire and they were trying to pull a burning barge from the water. It was far too heavy, and in spite of being a lot of people they had no hope. It was normal to paint the bottom and sides of the barges in pitch to make it watertight, but it also made it very flammable. I was soon to learn that something was very strange in that canal water, it didn't take long to burst into fire. It was soon blazing fiercely and all but the actual barge owner had abandoned it to its inevitable fate.

The three of us just stood and watched from our vantage point among the trees, high above the water.

"Maybe they will all go away," Sara said.

Father actually smiled as he said, "I don't think so, they have spent a hell of a lot of time, and money, to stop now."

I looked at him, as though he had returned from the dead, maybe Sara would come away now.

Almost to myself I said, "Water doesn't burn, it's not possible."

Even as I said it I was forced to admit the evidence was before my eyes, it was burning, not just the barge, it was the water itself.

The following day there were no barges on the canal, but lots of important people came and stood looking into its depth. They began ladling some of the water out. It's going to take a long while to get the water out that way, I thought.

Then some different workmen came and, using what I would learn was a pulley, managed to winch the remains of the barge onto dry land. It all seemed fascinating to me. I even went down to watch, taking care to seem to come from another direction. No one seemed interested in me. I even managed to talk to some of the workers, but I could hardly understand what they said. It was almost another language. But I did manage to find out what all the things were called.

I also found out that the important men were going to analyse the water to find out how it could burn. It seemed none of the workers had ever seen anything like it. They were all frightened of what would happen next.

Historical Facts.

From the start of the canal's operation, this trouble with fire in the water was a cause of great concern. One of the local mine owners had pumped some water out of his pit into the water, could it have come from there? A local brewery found that their water supply became contaminated, and numerous complaints were made to the canal owners. There is no evidence that anything was ever done for the brewers, or indeed for anyone else.

The help of a Professor Playfair of Manchester University, and a Doctor Young a noted distiller of petroleum, was sort and eventually Young set up a distillation works and was soon getting 300 gallons a day from his well. And so in 1847 the village of Riddings could lay claim to being the first inland petroleum producer in the country. Young made a considerable fortune and became known as Paraffin Young.

It would be a long while before any solution was found, and certainly not until three years after John's death. It was mainly coal from the many pits all over the commons, but some iron ore that wasn't used in the iron furnaces, coming from a seam said to be thirty feet thick, that was still transported along the canal highways.

The Butterley Company also moved its iron products the length of the country along the network. The great lake they had built in the hamlet of Butterley to top up the canal system, was now reinforced by another at Codnor Park. This wasn't far along from Ironville but on John's side of the canal system. No one knew if this was to give them more water to make the canal higher, or just to give cleaner water that wouldn't burn. The only people who knew why the lake was dug were the canal owners, and they didn't share that knowledge with anyone.

Then they began to chop down our trees, and it wouldn't be long before they joined up with the clearings that they called the Ryddings. Even father must realize our cott stood in the wrong place now. Even he must see it wouldn't be long before it was no more than a piece of burning wood on another blaze. It was our whole home and way of living that would be gone.

I decided the next day, after I had checked my traps and was happy with my yield, to go again to see my friends at the tannery. Surely they would understand my problems. They might even know of somewhere on the edge of the commons and yet just in the edge of the forest where we would be hidden, and so have the best of both worlds.

I took them a couple of rabbits, I didn't need anything in return, and I really wanted to talk to someone.

Martha was bending over the stove as I got to the house. "Would you like one of these?" I held them up for her.

She smiled at me. "The last lot were for treats, we can't afford them all the time."

"No, it's not like that. You helped me and I wanted to do something for you."

"I'll tell Thomas you are here. If he can get in, he'll like to see that you got back all right."

As she went I remembered the way the smell seemed to wrap its way all round the place. I'd almost forgotten, but now it seemed worse than ever.

Martha came back and said, "Thomas would like to see you, but he can't leave just now. He said go down and have a word."

"Thanks."

I went down. Those obnoxious vats with their stinking liquids were even worse as I got nearer. I saw a dead rat close by and wondered it the stink had killed it. This was indeed a hellhole, but Thomas and Martha were the nicest people you could meet. Maybe it was because not many people would go anywhere near them.

"Hello Thomas," I said. "I brought you a couple of rabbits for being my friend the other day."

He pulled the heavy skin of the beast on to the side before he spoke, "You don't have to keep bringing these for us you know."

"You did like them, they had only just been caught?"

"Yes they were great, I was just saying… "

As Thomas had appeared to stop, I said, "I wondered if you knew of any cotts that were in a good spot. It doesn't matter how bad a state they are in, I can always mend them. You know, on the edge of the woods, so we wouldn't be seen."

"I thought you had got the whole thing sorted."

"I did too, but someone has pulled the new place down, and they are starting to chop the trees down near the old one."

"Why?"

"Maybe it's something to do with the canal keep catching fire. Or it could be to do with pit props, so that the roof doesn't fall in on the miners."

"Water doesn't catch fire."

"This water does, come and see it if you don't believe me. Lot's of real gents keep coming to see it, and they have taken some water away. The bargeman said they are going to analyse it, then they will be able to stop it keep burning."

"I thought you didn't talk to anyone, you kept away from people."

"You can stand on the bank and talk to them, they can't grab you or anything."

Thomas smiled. "You don't seem to mind talking to me, I won't grab you or anything."

"You helped me, when you didn't have to. You are my friend, the only one I've got."

"It's nice to know someone likes me anyway, most folks keep clear of me because of the smell and all that."

Now I grinned. "I can't really say I like the smell either, but you are still my friend."

"I don't think I can help much anyway, I'm always working in the tannery, I just don't go walking round to see if any cotts are not in use."

"Sorry, I didn't think."

"If you got a job you could get some money and find a proper house."

"Like some of these round here?"

"Some of them are all right."

He knew that I was thinking of the unstable structures gracing the whole area.

Martha called, "I have just made a drink of herbal tea, if you want some."

Thomas said, "I can leave this for a bit now, so I'll have some with you."

We went down to the house and sat down on a bench. The tea was nice, it made me remember some mother used to make. We hadn't had any since she hadn't been there any more.

With the skins pulled down across the door this place was very cosy. Either I was getting accustomed to the smell, or the skins somehow masked it, I don't know, but it didn't seem so bad now.

We talked a while about what was happening at the canal, and the worry about the trees. I told them about my new cott I had built in the birch wood being pulled down. And how I had found the three ponds with the fish, and that I had an idea to make a sort of net with thin willow branches on the end of a birch pole. This was something that had come into my mind as I talked about the pond. It could work, in fact there was no reason for it not to work. I had managed to catch a fish, even if I couldn't hold it, so providing the fish couldn't get through the holes, I would have it. I certainly knew how to weave the willow round, and make the holes as small as I wanted them. It was just the same as when I made the framework for the new cott and how I did it with the new bed.

Thomas said, "I know the ponds, though I haven't been to them for years, they call them Penny-town ponds."

Seemingly still thinking about what I had said about the net,

"It's a good idea," he began thoughtfully, continuing, "but you must be very careful. Anyone sitting there for ages trying to get fish won't like it if you come with your mesh and scoop them all out."

"Nobody owns them, who can stop me?" I said, petulantly.

Thomas was smiling. "I never said you hadn't the right but remember, when you had your new coat those men tried to take it from you. They will take your fish as well, and your new net."

"So you don't think I could do it?"

"I think you should be very careful. Maybe if you went around the back end, the woods always were very thick round there, no one would notice you in the trees. And when you have one or two, get away quickly so no one knows just what you have been doing."

Martha gave me another cup of her tea.

"I will give you the first fish I catch, just for being my friends."

My mind was full of my new idea.

Thomas said, "I've been here long enough, I must get back to the vats. We haven't all got such an easy life as you have. If most folks don't work, they don't eat."

I bid them both goodbye and stood outside their place, wondering if I should explore further round Alfreton. There seemed so much to see, but then I would have plenty of time another day. I walked down the hill following the line of the drainage to the horse-wash pond. I was on the opposite side from where I had been before so I could cut across the commons, all the time keeping to the high ground, until I reached the Greenhill track that snaked its way past the Ryddings. Then into the woods and down the slope till I reached our cott.

As I had been walking back, I thought about what Thomas had said. I thought about the bargemen, and their women and kids, covered in the grime of their coal, or whatever else they happened to be carrying. I thought about the black-faced miners, trudging like robots, carrying their picks and shovels over their shoulders, afraid to put them down in case someone stole them. They went along the canal edge with scarcely the energy to look round them. Did they even know if the sun ever shone? I wondered did they ever think, and scheme, about what they would do next?

And then Thomas himself. He seemed to have a nice house, better that the cotts anyway, but he had to spend every hour of the day in that stinking tannery.

I had never known father to work. Oh yes, he set the traps, just the same I do, he knew just where to find the berries, or the herbs. All my life I had never known what it was to be hungry, even in the middle of the snows of winter. We had the thick covers over the bed and Mother made coats for us all from the rabbit skins.

I checked the traps and got another rabbit. Yes, we always had plenty of food.

I went and looked to see if there was any other excitement by the canal. It seemed very quiet, then I saw that the barges were moored a little further down. That was good, the further away from us the better. There were quite a few people talking to each other down by the barges, but still they didn't seem to be coming any further.

No one had chopped down any more of our trees.

I went back to our cott, still thinking about my new fish catching net. It seemed so easy, I wondered why no one had done it before. A long stick wasn't needed, so I could either carry it, or even leave it hidden by the pond. If I could take the net off the end no one could possibly know what it was for, and if I lost it I could soon make another.

Father still seemed in his own world, with Sara just content to wait on him. I just couldn't understand her, what had he ever done for either of us?

The next day I was up at first light. I broke a small branch off a birch tree, trimmed it down, then got a thinner piece of willow and twisted it back into a loop. Next, I bound them together round the bottom of my birch branch, then with some smaller, even more pliable willow I fastened the whole lot together. Now I had a fish net, I left it to one side to let the wood get accustomed to its new tension. I knew from experience that wood sometimes breaks if it isn't given time to get used to being fastened in an unusual way. In a little while I would retighten the thing. Then I could weave some more willow around the gaps, then and only then would I be able to test the effectiveness of my brand new fish catcher.

I felt excited, as I wanted to see if it would work, but these things cannot be rushed. Then, and only then, there would be nothing to stop me catching just as many fish as I wanted.

I felt proud of my new invention, but I was also wary, I could understand people wouldn't like it if I caught all their fish, especially if they had sat trying to get them for hours.

After a trip to check my snares I found I hadn't caught any animals, rabbits or anything, then I checked the barges. Nothing seemed to be moving on the canal so I went back to the cott.

I got hold of my fishing net, and having decided the thing was substantial enough to do the job, I began to weave other willow strands in and out of the net, so that the holes were tight enough to stop the bigger fish escaping, and the thing was strong enough to hold them. Then I set off.

I was very excited, after all this was my invention. I thought no one had made a fish catcher like this before.

I stationed myself at the third, and largest pond, at the opposite side to where I had seen the man fishing with his stick. The trees were thick so that no one would see me, not that I saw anyone around, and I settled myself down and waited. It wasn't quite as easy as I thought, every time I swished my net through the water to scoop a fish it made so many ripples that all the fish kept far away for a long time afterwards, and I seemed to be waiting for ages. Luckily I had brought my thick coat because it was getting cold, and frankly I wasn't used to just sitting waiting. Eventually I scooped up quite a big fish, and immediately afterwards I got another. I wasn't going to stop any longer, it was getting too close to winter and wasn't the time of year to sit still. I could feel my teeth chattering, but still the two fish were quite a good catch. I would have to get some sort of lure to get them to swim into the net.

My idea was good, but it would take me a while to perfect my technique. Thankfully I could walk back without leaving the woods, so no one would be likely to see me. By the time I got back, the brisk walk had brought the circulation back to my limbs. And I was feeling pretty pleased with myself.

Sara cleaned and cooked the fish, as though she had been doing it all her life, and we had a nice change from the meat, usually rabbit, that was our staple diet.

Afterwards, after checking to see that there was nothing happening around the canal, I found myself falling asleep, by the fire in the cott.

Later, I went down to the canal, by my roundabout route of course. They seemed to have stopped chopping the trees down and I saw the man I had spoken to before.

"Have they found out why the water keeps burning?" I asked him.

"No idea, but we aren't going to go any further down there, not until we know it's safe."

"Have they stopped chopping the trees down now?"

"I think they were for the pit props, and they are mostly too thin."

There was a silence before the bargeman spoke again.

"Just look what happened to Harry Blant's barge." He indicated the burnt out hulk now standing where it had been pulled, on the edge of the water. "That will remind everyone what happened, no one will risk it."

"It's terrible," I agreed. But secretly I thought, good, you lot might go away now. "Will they shut the canal down then?"

"Oh no, they've spent too much money on it. We want them to build another wharf, a bit further down, so we can load where it's safe."

"See you," I said, as he made his way along the canal bank.

It looked as if we would have to live with the canal because it was going to stay, and the cessation of traffic was no more than a temporary reprieve. It seemed to me more important than ever to find a new cott.

I followed the canal down towards the big works at Butterley. I had known something big was happening, now I saw it, the company was building a new furnace for iron ore smelting. This was as well as the two they already had.

There was always something else happening along the waterway. The whole area was getting bigger and there was more and more industry. Was it like this everywhere? Soon there wouldn't be any trees, and no more rabbits to eat. What would happen then? Everybody would starve.

The biting wind was picking up again, there was snow and sleet and it was not yet December, this was going to be a harsh winter. I wished I had brought my new coat and the thought made me smile. Not many people had got a coat, certainly not kids, they had to rough it. "Thickens the blood," father said. I decided that I would prefer thin blood.

Chapter 3

Sara continued to tell me that she wouldn't leave the cott without father, so I didn't make a lot of effort to find another place for us to live, especially as they seemed to have stopped chopping the trees down. Perhaps because they were mostly saplings and not suitable for pit props, as the man said. However, I did continue to explore further around the area, I hadn't given up entirely on the idea.

I also went into Alfreton on some Tuesdays, which was market day, keeping an eye out for the men who tried to rob me. I didn't see them though. There didn't seem anything that we needed, so I didn't get a thing. I gave my friends at the tannery another couple of rabbits. They offered me all sorts of things in return. I just said when I thought of anything I wanted, I'd tell them.

Then I went up to the church, I'd become fascinated with the place, I'd never seen anything as big in my life. I saw the man in the strange white robes and he showed me around inside. I asked him who lived there and he said no one. It was a place where people came to pray to God, or just to sit in the quiet with their own thoughts, and told me to come on Sundays. It all seemed so strange.

I made my way down behind the town and stood looking at the horse-wash pond. I thought I couldn't imagine anyone washing horses in it, it stunk of urine. Then, taking care to keep to the high ground, I made my way back across the commons and so back to our cott. On the way back I saw they had started to build a huge, square-shaped brick building, halfway along the Lea Lane. I was looking at it when one of the builders saw me.

"Careful they never stick you inside one of these places lad."

"What is it?"

"It's going to be a workhouse, where they put people who have got no money, or work, then they work 'em to death."

I gave an involuntary shudder and quickly walked on. I could be described as having no money or work, but I could keep a useless father and Sara well enough fed. I could build a new cott, and invent my own new fish catcher, why did I need money? It was on my mind as I made my way back to the cott.

The winter of 1806/7 came early and was the harshest in living memory. By the end of November we had our first sprinkling of snow then, within a week of the beginning of December the straight depth was more than a foot, with drifts in places more than four feet deep. Then came the frosts, a crispy top covering that sometimes gave way, dropping an unwary walker in a big hole.

I still caught some rabbits, though they hadn't much meat on their bones. I found that I could catch more squirrels now because with the snow covering they didn't seem to realize the traps were there, whilst in decent weather they dodged them far better than the rabbits.

Because the cutting wind blew through the trees, which were mainly on the higher ground, the snow had been blown down in the direction of the canal. So there was still sparse vegetation for rabbits, and any other herbivore that still survived among the conditions. We managed well enough. The cott was warm and well insulated against the winter's blasts, and we had father's coat as well as mine to wrap around us, and our body heat kept us cosy enough, even in the winter.

The canal froze over. Because the water didn't flow as in rivers, it froze quickly. Men with big hammers smashed the ice. If they couldn't get the barges moving, they couldn't earn anything. I had gone down to see what was happening and the canal man I knew gave me a hammer so I could help. Once they got going, the weight of the barges kept the ice broken and the water free. As each vessel followed the next, the whole lot was kept churned up. I imagined the same chaos would happen every night, and every place they stopped at, so long as this weather continued. If it got a lot colder, I imagined they really would be in real trouble, after all the winter had barely begun.

I thought about Sara. When she had to go outside she would face the inclement weather without the benefit of anything to keep her warm. I resolved to try to get out to see Thomas and Martha, I could spare perhaps a couple of rabbits, skinny as they were, and a squirrel. Between them they would provide some sustenance. I thought of numb fingers trying to drag the skin of some beast to the edge of the vat. Then I wondered if the cold weather would in some way kill the smell.

Perhaps if they were getting hungry enough they would think even this meagre morsel would be worth something, enough anyway, to keep Sara warm.

If I went through the woods to the Ryddings I would be keeping mainly to the higher ground and it would be safe. I wouldn't risk it if the conditions became too bad.

I stood looking down between the trees and I could see the barges were still moving. Along the canal edge the zombies still trudged their weary way along the banks. One way their faces black, making their way back from the mines, the other way something akin to clean. They still looked worn out and beaten before they started their twelve hours with a pick and shovel hacking the black stuff from the bowels of the earth. Men, women and children, all with the same black faces, and zombie expressions.

Would any of them know how to build a place to live in, could they catch food, from the forests, or feel the weather, the sun and wind and yes, even the snow?

I pitied them.

I turned my mind back to the task in hand. The skies looked full of snow, the risk was there, but on the whole I thought it was worth it, for everyone's sake.

Sara looked at me as I put on my coat. "The traps, or fishing?" she asked.

She rarely questioned where I was going.

"Neither, I want to make a trade."

"Be careful, we might have some more snow." I looked at her, and she added, "I was just concerned."

"Thank you Sis. I wouldn't go, but I think it's necessary."

I went and put my arm round her for the first time since mother died. She shrugged me off.

"Don't be daft."

I could get there and back in less than two hours normally. I went through the wood up to the Ryddings, past one or two houses, and on to the track they call the Greenhill. I almost crossed it, there was nothing to show where it was, but I realised at the last minute, then I trudged on through the snow. In places it was very deep, I fell once or twice, and had a lot of difficulty getting up once. I couldn't get anything for leverage, but after what seemed a long time, I managed to get out of the hole. I admit I was starting to get frightened and when I finally got out, I stood wondering if I ought to go back, but I had the rabbits and I was halfway there. I continued, trying to keep to the places where the snow had been blown away. After a while I saw the start of Alfreton and the snow had been trodden down a bit. I felt grateful to get to the tannery.

"What on earth are you doing here? It's likely going to snow again," said Thomas.

I tried to grin from sheer bravado.

"I thought you must be getting ready for some rabbits, and a squirrel, and I wanted to do a trade." I undid my coat. "I'm afraid they aren't very good ones, but there isn't a lot of food about for them either. And it's for Sara, she has nothing to keep her warm in this lot."

"Didn't you hear about Ted Brown?"

"I don't know Ted Brown, in fact I don't know anyone but you, Martha and Sara. Oh, and father, but he's nobody."

Thomas looked at me as though in reproach but didn't follow up.

He said, "Ted Brown tried to walk not more than one hundred yards, from the pub to his own house, you would have thought he would have known where all the likely trouble spots were. It seemed he didn't and the snow gave way under him. He fell into a snow hole, he couldn't get out and they found him next day frozen solid, he'd died of frostbite."

"I'm sorry."

He looked at me. "Are you all right? You look as if you have seen a ghost, are you sure you didn't know him? Anyway sit down, Martha will make you some herbal tea."

I realised just how much trouble I'd had in the hole I fell in, and that wasn't that deep. I tried to grin.

"I'll have to be quick, I'll have to get back as soon as I can. It took me a lot longer than usual to get here, and the last thing I need is to be caught in the dark, I might not see any holes either."

"We can make you a bed here."

"There's no guarantee it'll be any better tomorrow, and Sara will be worried."

"I hope she knows what you are doing for her."

"That doesn't matter, so long as I can get something to keep her warm."

Martha had come down from the house, and when she saw me she said, "You shouldn't turn out in this weather. I'll make you a tea." She turned and walked back.

Thomas grinned. "I told you she would make you a tea, it's her standard for everything."

I followed her into the house and Thomas came up as well, no doubt glad to take a break.

I had the drink, which warmed me, and Martha brought me a smaller coat that would fit Sara just great. I noticed Thomas and Martha exchange glances and I said, "I know the rabbits weren't very good, but you did say you owed me something for the last lot I brought. I'll bring you some more if that's it."

"No, you don't have to do that."

I looked from one to the other.

Martha said, "It was one Thomas did for me, but I've got others, and it seems that Sara really needs it."

"She's right," Thomas said. "I'm sorry, and you did risk life and limb to get here."

"I don't want to make any trouble."

"Don't be daft, you thought about us and that's nice."

They seemed all right now and I said, "I saw an axe down by the vat. I wonder if I could borrow it just for a few minutes to chop a sapling down. I think a stick would help me on the way back, in case I fall in a hole like that other chap. What did you say his name was?"

"Ted Brown, and yes of course you can."

Thomas walked back with me to the vats and handed me the axe. I was eyeing a group of small trees just behind the building.

"I think that small branch will be all right, if you don't mind."

"Yes of course. Do you want me to chop it for you?"

"No, I'm used to doing things like this all the time."

I chopped the branch off, taking it with the grain, trimmed it down until it suited my purpose, then handed him back his axe.

Thomas said, "You handled that well, for a young boy."

"As I said, I do it all the time, wood for the fire, and different things we need."

"If you have time some day, when the weather gets better, would you like to chop down some of that cluster? It'll give me more light, and some wood for the fire."

"It'll be my pleasure, but not today, I must get back before dark."

I was looking up at the sky, and it didn't look good. The day hadn't really come properly light. Thomas tried again to make me stop for the night, but I knew I had to get back. Anyway I had a little more confidence now that I had a sturdy stick.

I went back the same way as I had come. Once outside the houses I could feel that the wind had picked up, that was bad news, it would blow the loose-lying snow into what holes there were, making it more dangerous. I had my new stick though, so that I could prod anything I wasn't sure of.

The fact was, the frost had solidified the snow a bit, and it hadn't blown as much as it might have. I made quite good progress really, but the light, already not too good, was starting to fade noticeably as I pulled off the Greenhill track and up over the Ryddings, but I hadn't far to go now. Still, I had stumbled a time or two but my stick helped me to keep my balance, and the one time I actually fell it was useful in regaining my feet.

I was glad to eventually see the cott and Sara standing by the door.

"Go inside, you will be frozen, or at least put this on." I handed her the new warm coat.

She took the coat, but seemed more concerned about father than herself. She said, "It's father, he doesn't look at all well, and I can't get him warm."

He looked exactly the same to me. He hadn't looked more than half alive since he had killed mother and made us all watch.

"Shall I fetch the wise woman?" Sara asked.

"No you shouldn't, she wouldn't come on a night like this anyway. I'll build the fire up and we can all get warm, tomorrow we will see what's the best thing to do."

I certainly wouldn't let Sara go to fetch anyone, and I'd no idea where the wise woman lived.

I built up the fire, put a pile of the small logs nearby and I pulled the cover over the entrance. It was as warm and snug as could be.

I'd noticed that it was starting to snow as I had brought in the final armful of logs, and was already quite dark. As usual, I covered the fire with some turf, which kept the fire smouldering and therefore the heat. No fear of setting fire to anything, and no fear of burning out. It was cosy and as warm as any other house on that night.

I realized I'd only just got back in time. In the dark, and snow, I would have had no chance.

We got father into bed. Sara slept next to father and I on the outside. When all of us had been together it had been father and mother, then the younger ones in order, which put Sara as the eldest on the outside. Now I had confiscated the outside spot, on the pretext that it would need to be me who got up in any emergency. That was what I had said, in reality I wanted to be as far from that man as I could.

I began to shiver, and it wasn't just the cold. Ted Brown was less than a hundred yards from his own house. How would Sara have managed? I wouldn't be taking any chances like that in future.

I found I couldn't stop myself trembling. Sara pulled herself close to my back, and I heard her say, "I'm sorry, I know that you did it for me, but I was worried."

Gradually my limbs calmed down. The warmth, the feeling of safety and, in a way, the sound of the wind gradually rising and we were warm, settled me. Then, with the natural resilience of youth, I slept.

I was wet when I awoke and had obviously been sweating quite a bit. Sara was already up she had warmed some stew over the fire.

"Have some of this, it'll make you feel better."

I realized that to get up she must have crept over me, but I hadn't even noticed.

We had some pieces of towel which father had bartered from the market once, so I towelled myself down before putting something dry on. Only then, sitting down on the edge of the bed, did I have some of the warm, refreshing stew.

Sara said, "I was worried, you were thrashing about so much, and shouting and moaning. I dried you down once, you didn't seem to even notice."

"I'm sorry Sis, must have got a bit colder than I thought," I said, sheepishly.

"But you wouldn't wake up."

"Do you like your coat?"

"It's warm, I'm so lucky. But are you sure you are all right? You didn't wake up at all yesterday."

"I must have, anyway I feel all right."

"What with you, and father."
"Oh, him."

"I did get him to have some stew, he seems a bit better."
"I'll go and see if I can net some fish today. It'll make a change."

"You wouldn't be able to get there. In fact the whole cott is covered with snow. It's about four feet deep, I had to dig some away from the door."

"But how did you get some water?"

"I melted some snow."

"How did you know it would be all right to drink?"

"I tried some myself, so I knew it would."

"Oh Sara."

After the stew I dressed myself up warm and went outside. It really did look a sea of whiteness, but as we were on the very top of the hill, some had blown away just from the around the crest. It was really a sight to behold, but now it was crunchy underfoot, and it was very cold. No more was likely to go until it began to thaw. I remember father saying once, "It won't snow any more if it gets too cold."

I went to where I could see the canal. The boats seemed to be stopped, stuck in a sea of whiteness, but they still hadn't gone any further up the water. Seemed they still thought it would catch fire, though I would have thought there was enough snow to stop that happening.

There wasn't any other activity, then quite suddenly, as if by some prearranged signal, the zombies started to trudge along the bank. Men, women and children, all with the same black faces and robot-like movements.

The snow was well worn away on the canal edge, so a lot of boots had continuously trampled it away.

I looked in the direction of the three ponds. There wasn't any sign of indentations in the snow in that direction, and I wasn't risking being another Ted Brown.

We had enough rabbits to keep us fed, even if they weren't very good ones, but there would be no herbs to season them. Still we would have to do.

I went back inside and saw to the fire. We were comfortable enough, with enough wood inside that was dry. I could chop some more, long before we ran out.

Sara said, "Who is Ted Brown?"

"I don't know, why?"

"You were moaning about him in your sleep."

As Sara seemed to want more of an answer, I said I had been told he was just someone who had died in the snow.

"And you still went out didn't you?"

"I didn't know then, Sis."

"I couldn't look after father if anything happened to you."

"Father, father, you always seem to be more bothered about him than anything."

"He is our father."

"And what about mother, he didn't care about her, he killed her and made us watch."

"He didn't know what would happen, he just thought it would be all right."

We wouldn't agree about him, so better not to talk at all.

I went outside, no more snow had fallen, and only the bits on the very crest of the hill looked safe. Elsewhere the snow looked pristine, and dangerous. I went and checked the traps. They were mainly on the very crest of the hill, but nothing else had fallen prey and I wondered if every local animal had starved to death.

If I really had slept all day yesterday, I couldn't remember two days together when nothing had been caught. It was odd and somehow frightening.

I went back into our cott. It was warm, there was plenty of logs, nothing to worry about for a long time yet. We had enough meat for a good few days as well. But I went a way along the crest and chopped some logs just to give myself something to do. We never chopped anything down that was near to our cott because we always wanted to keep as much cover as possible. There never had been many people close to us, but with all the new activity all around we seemed somehow more vulnerable now than ever before.

The next day I decided to risk trying for some fish, it was probably about a mile to the three ponds. I was well wrapped up against the elements, I had my stick to probe any risky spots, and I could always get up with the stick if I fell. But the snow came above my knees in a lot of places, it was certainly the worst I had ever known.

I made it to the ponds. They were covered with a layer of snow and it was hard to tell just where the water started, but I scraped a clear spot close to the bank. The ice wasn't as thick as I expected, just a covering, so I dragged my stick through the water and quickly made an opening. Now that I'd managed to make a clear spot I settled with my back to the same tree that I had used the last time. The snow seemed pristine over the whole pond and the banks, apart from my spot.

Now with my net into the water I sat and waited, watching the water for the telltale ripples as the fish swam by. I would soon have some fish now, that was what I thought, and I was very wrong. I waited and waited for a very long time, hidden under the trees at the far side of the pond, with my net ready, until the inclement weather seemed to eat its way through even the warmth of my new coat, and I found my teeth chattering and my bones numb. I found my mind thinking of poor Ted Brown who had frozen to death.

Even after my ordeal, I neither caught nor indeed saw a single fish. Normally there were lots of them swimming near to the surface, but they weren't. I never saw one and that was a fact.

I went back very disheartened, and not a little frightened.

If I couldn't catch rabbits, and now I couldn't catch fish, how could we live?

I made my way through the twichel, on to the higher ground of the Ryddings and back towards our cott. My feet were wet and I felt colder than I had ever been in my whole life.

I had to walk past the traps so I checked each one, and was surprised to find that I had caught a wild dog. The thing was snarling and baring its fangs, but as it was stuck it wasn't in any position to harm me. I approached it from one side, calmly raised my stick and took careful aim. Two sharp cracks about its head with my new stick soon quietened it down. Apart from a few twitches it didn't move again, it was meat.

I waited a while, making sure it wasn't going to come round, but its head seemed battered in. I got some willow twigs, tied them around its feet and found that the snow was useful. It slid easily as I dragged it across the surface, unfortunately though it was leaving a trail of blood. Still, I hadn't got far to go and I could go back and cover my tracks.

Sara would soon skin it and get it in the pot, so that if it did happen to have an owner, it would be long gone and no one would be the wiser.

The dog in a strange way calmed me down. I admit I was starting to become frightened, in the same way that I had when I had fallen in the snow coming back from Alfreton and not known if I would ever get back. Now it was while I was wondering if we would ever find anything else to eat, there was no one else to get food, it all depended on me.

At seven years of age I had already got the thinking mentality as an adult.

Sis had cooked another rabbit when I got back. I dropped the dog by the door, put my net away, and after a quick reconnaissance of my pathway and the covering of any blood with snow, I went inside and settled down.

The weather was very, very cold, but no more snow had fallen.

I took my trousers off and hung them so that they would dry. I towelled my legs down and I could feel the circulation gradually coming back, as though the blood was starting to move again in my legs.

We were warm enough in the cott though, and gradually my limbs stopped twitching as the heat took away my ordeal. Then suddenly, unexplainably I began to sweat. It was an uncontrollable thing. I began to shake again and had difficulty in even eating my rabbit. Then Sara helped to towel me down again and she insisted I went to bed.

As I lay there I noticed that Sara was spoon-feeding father. I'm sure I wouldn't have. If he wouldn't eat, then he could starve as far as I was concerned.

Then, with the warmth of the cott I fell into a sound sleep.

I dreamed a strange, mixed-up dream about a man in a hole and trying to get him out. Then I was in that hole, the man laughing at me and walking away. Then there was Sara, standing at the cott, but she was just skin and bones. I hadn't come back so she had nothing to eat. Then there was Martha coming, and taking her coat back, saying, "It's my coat and I want it back."

The canal was on fire again, big flames.

Sara had her arms round me, cradling my head in her lap. She was saying, "It's all right, I won't let anything hurt you."

"What's happening Sis?"

"Just be quiet, you are all right now." Her hand was caressing my face. "You had a bad dream that's all."

I was drifting in and out of sleep, conscious of the fact that Sara was feeding me from time to time. Suddenly it was another hand that was holding my neck and offering something into my mouth. I swallowed some evil-tasting liquid. Instantly my eyes were open and I was looking into those piercing black eyes of the wise woman. I tried to struggle away from her but she was far stronger than I was.

I tried to say something but it must have been incoherent. She lowered my head back on to the bed. I could even hear her speaking, but somehow I hadn't the strength to reply, or even to raise myself up from my prone position. I tried again to say something, but could utter no more than a croak.

The wise woman said, "I think the fever had broken now, he will sleep. If he wakes in the next couple of hours, give him some more of this, then just let him sleep it off. He will be weak, but should be all right now."

I heard her clearly enough, I could see her standing next to Sara. I tried to move myself, I couldn't lie here for long, I would soon have to catch some food, one way or another, or we would all starve. I even thought like an adult now. Something was very wrong, I couldn't move. My body was too heavy and my arms just weren't strong enough to lift me. I even saw Sara give her a couple of our rabbits. What was she doing, we couldn't have many left.

Eventually I woke. It was dark and Sara was lying next to me. Was she asleep, was it the start of the night, or nearing dawn? I lay there quietly. There was no point in trying to get up. I must wait until first light. I closed my eyes. I might as well sleep. In the daylight I could make my plans.

Chapter 4

I don't know how long I lay in my delirium. The snow had already gone. We hadn't starved. It seemed I wasn't as important as I thought. It was Sara who had set the traps and caught anything that was unwary. Sara who invented a way to travel across the snow. She had used the willows in the same way that I had made my fish net and made some snowshoes that could walk on top of the snow. It was Sara who had spoon-fed me back to health.

When I returned to normality, and took my first shaky steps, I could only marvel that a girl could do so much.

"I owe you my life Sis."

"Not me," she said. "It is Miriam you have to thank."

"Miriam, who, or what, is Miriam?"

"Miriam is the wise woman. She sat with you, it wasn't me, and she made the potions that broke the fever."

"How did you manage to get to her in all that snow, and how did you get her to come?"

"I just told her that you were ill, and how you had tried to keep the family fed, and how you got me such a lovely warm coat. I told her I would give her the coat if she made you better."

"I will get you another coat."

"Oh, she didn't take it, I just gave her some rabbits and a fox."

I was sitting on the edge of the bed. Suddenly, there were tears starting to stream down my face and I couldn't stop them. Sara passed the towel.

"I'm sorry Sis," I said, as I tried to hide my face.

"It's all right John. Maybe we both have had to grow up a bit too quickly," she said, thoughtfully. "Miriam said we shouldn't have to stay here on our own, but then when she saw how we managed, I think she thought we got on better than a lot of grown-ups."

I said, "Do you think Miriam would like a coat?"

"She will if we get any more snow like the last lot."

"I'll try to get her one."

"You will have to get a lot stronger before you go anywhere."

"I suppose so."

"By the way, I know what happened to Ted Brown, Miriam told me. Did you actually see him then?"

"No, I was just told."

"But it seemed to affect you so much."

"No, not really. I just thought that if a grown man couldn't get up out of a snow hole."

"I told you not to go."

"I thought I had to be the grown-up, now I know that I can't manage without you Sis. In future we will do things together, then we can do anything."

"Just remember, both of us are really just kids."

"I think you are something more than an ordinary kid Sis."

"Don't be daft."

The next few days I concentrated on getting stronger again. It was Sara who went out and came back with the rabbits.

One day I asked her what the dog tasted like and she just smiled. "I skinned it and I cooked it, but Miriam took it. I said I didn't fancy dog so she took it. She said it was nice though."

We just laughed together.

I'd been outside and checked the wood store. Sara had even chopped a new pile of that. I walked along the crest of the hill until I could see the canal, and the barges were moving along, but they still didn't come up to the wharf. The barges seemed to be loading further along the bank, so they were still frightened about the fires.

When I came back in I was wondering about the fish. Had the snow really killed them all off?

"What were you thinking about?" Sara asked, suddenly.

"How do you know I was thinking about anything?"

"It's the look on your face when you are trying to think things out."

"It was just the fish," I said.

"Oh, they are all right."

"How do you know, you haven't been catching fish as well have you?"

"No, Miriam asked why you had gone out. She said we had enough meat so why had you gone trampling in the snow and water like that? She thought you had been very silly, then she told me that fish swim deeper in nasty weather."

It was in my mind to retort, what's it got to do with her? But I thought better of it.

"I suppose she was right."

The next day the wise woman arrived, I still couldn't bring myself to give her any name. Sara was talking and giggling with her in a way she never talked to me. I felt somehow cut out. She asked me how I was, almost as an afterthought.

When she eventually went, Sara gave her a couple of rabbits, with no consultation with me. I wouldn't admit it, but more than ever I felt left out.

Sara said, "Miriam has left some more of that potion to make you get better."

"What, to knock me out for another day or two?" I said, petulantly.

"No, to make you better, and I've get some other for father."

"What can you possibly do for him?"

Everything seemed about Miriam or father.

It turned very cold during the night and a heavy frost covered everything by morning. The next day it didn't warm up at all and the bargemen were using their big hammers to break the ice. Then after a few days it warmed slightly and the snow came down, deeper than before. Still Sara managed to get enough meat for us to manage. It was cosy enough inside the cott, and Sara still insisted I stayed inside.

Then one day father died. He looked just the same as he had done since he killed mother, but Sara seemed to know. She set off on her snow shoes to fetch the wise woman, who came and was followed by two men who took him away in a cart. Though how the donkey managed to pull that cart through the snow I don't know.

He was taken to Alfreton church and they buried him in a pauper's grave, by the iron railings, just inside the church grounds.

It seemed that Alfreton was the only place within a six-mile radius that anyone could be buried. Miriam said she had seen that he was put in the same spot as mother and she made a little board with a cross. It read: William and Elizabeth Barlow. RIP. And she stuck it over them.

"I wasn't supposed to do that," she said, "but I did. The Reverend Pepper knows me well enough; he insists his housekeeper sends for me when he's not very well. He swears that my herbs cure him quicker than the doctor ever can."

She was smiling at the thought, then turning back to us she said that she would show us where they were when the snow had gone.

I was intrigued by their names. I don't think I had heard them before. They were just father and mother. It seemed father was twenty-nine years old and mother had been only twenty-four. All this the wise woman could tell us. I didn't ask her how she knew this.

Sara was very quiet, she didn't want to talk to me at all, but with Miriam she chattered all the time, it seemed that they were the best of friends. What had I done?

After a while I put on my coat and went outside, they didn't seem to notice that I had left.

The next day Sara told me Miriam was going to teach her about herbs so that she could cure the sick and know what helped with pain. "I will be able to help women when they were having babies. I will be a sort of apprentice and people will be able to send for me."

"But you are only a kid," I blurted out, and immediately wished I hadn't.

"I am older than you, and you seem to think you are grown-up."

"I'm sorry Sis, I shouldn't have said that."

"No, you shouldn't, and you shouldn't keep blaming father, he didn't know what would happen to mother."

"I said I was sorry."

"It was father you should have told, he might be here now if you had."

I hadn't realized that was how Sara felt, but from that moment there seemed to be a bigger rift between us. And to make matters worse, we both realised that she didn't need me now. Everything that I could do Sara could do just as well.

When I had been ill it had been Sara who had kept the home together, I thought. It was me who had made the fishing net, but that wasn't much good if the weather was bad. Sara had made the snowshoes, and they were the same principle so she could make a net to.

I would have to be very careful now. She was already talking about helping Miriam with the herbs, even delivering babies. Soon she would be the wise woman. I felt worried. Everything I had ever planned included Sara. What if she went? What would happen then?

It began to snow again, big flakes that settled on the frozen ground. This time it didn't stop, it snowed all the rest of that day, and the next. In fact, there were very few days during the next six weeks when it didn't snow. I made myself some snowshoes like Sara's, but just how thick the snow was I couldn't tell. The canal was thick with the stuff, the barges were still, no amount off hammering could break the ice, and everything stopped.

I found I could move quite well, over the top, but I couldn't catch anything. Sara had built up a food store so we were all right for a while. She even took some to her friend Miriam. I dare not utter a word of protest.

I did manage to catch a fox one day, and one rabbit, but it was a mangy thing. We were still all right, so I took it to Thomas and Martha at the tannery. I wondered if I could get something warm for the wise woman. I had to try to build bridges, or I was going to lose Sara.

They were surprised to see me, told me they had been worried about how I had been in all the snow, and they were fascinated with my snowshoes. I told them about how I had been ill, and the way Sara had saved me. I told them about the wise woman, and then how Sara blamed me for what had happened to father.

"I've got to try to do something to make things right with Sis. I'm frightened the wise woman will take Sara away from me. She wants to teach her to be a wise woman as well."

They knew the wise woman. She had helped Martha once.

"Sara seems to be quite a clever girl, and I can see why Miriam would like to have her, but she wouldn't leave you."

"She would, she hates me for what happened to father."

Nobody spoke for a while, then I blurted out, "I have come to ask a special favour. If you say no, it will be all right, I'll understand, and I'll still think of you as my very best friends."

Thomas smiled. "We won't know what you want if you don't ask."

I looked from one to the other. "I want to do a trade, but I have nothing much to offer."

I opened my coat to show them the fox and the skinny rabbit.

"I'll bring you some more as soon as the weather breaks."

"And you want what?" Martha asked, not unkindly.

"Sara offered her coat to the wise woman so that she would help me."

"And now you want to get Sara another one?"

"Yes, and no. The wise woman didn't take it. Sara told her I had caught the fever trying to catch some food to keep her and father fed. She wouldn't take a thing, and she kept coming in all that weather, until she knew I was all right."

"Now she wants Sara as a sort of payment?"

"No. She just tells her about her life, and how she will teach her to be a wise woman. And Sara hates me for what happened to father, and they just laugh and chat together all the time."

"And you feel left out? It's only natural that Sara likes to be with another woman sometimes."

"Perhaps, but what if she goes?"

"What do you really want?"

"I want to be able to give that woman a coat for herself, then she will have been paid, and maybe she will leave Sara alone."

Thomas and Martha exchanged glances. "I'm sorry John, but it doesn't work like that. If she really wants to go she will, and there is nothing you or anyone can do about it."

"You won't help me then?"

"We will help you, in any way we can," Thomas said.

"I know the fox and that rabbit aren't worth much, but I promise I will repay my debts, whatever you say I owe you."

"I'll give you another of my coats," Martha said. "But don't think you can keep Sara for ever, because you can't. What I can make of Sara, she is like you, grown-up far too soon. She will do what she wants, and neither a coat nor anything else will stop her."

I took the coat back and told Sara it was for Miriam. It was for what she had done for our family.

Sara looked hard at me. "I know what you are trying to do, John."

She was becoming very perceptive, as though she understood me, more than I did myself.

"I thought you would like her to have the coat, that's all."

"It would be a very nice thought, but you don't like Miriam do you?"

"I haven't thought about her."

She looked away from me.

"Please Sara, I just want us to be family again."

"You resented me trying to help father to get well, you just wanted to leave him. Now you resent me having a friend."

"I don't Sara, it's just that everything seems to be breaking up, and I can't stop it."

"You have always done just what you want and expected me to agree. Well I won't, not every time anyway."

"I got you the coat, I didn't want you to get cold, and now I've got one for Miriam."

"Yes, and that was very nice, but don't think you know what I want, ask me first."

"I will Sara, yes I will."

Things settled down after that. We caught some rabbits, but not many, and they were very poor specimens. We had a store of food so we managed well enough.

I didn't get down to see my friends at the tannery. I was conscious of the fact that I still owed them some meat, and I had promised to cut down the trees for Thomas, but the snow was showing little sign of thawing. Even with the snowshoes it was still difficult, but certainly not impossible to get about. Sara took the coat to the wise woman. I was worried in case she didn't come back, but she did.

The barges started to move, but soon came to a halt again. For a while even the zombies stopped their continuous march. There was a large stock of the black stuff piled up by the edge of the canal. It the barges didn't move the coal then there wasn't much point in mining it.

The days had started to get a little longer before the snow eventually started to go. It had been a long hard winter. But the bargemen had finally broken the ice and they began the task of reducing the stockpile of coal. Gradually normality returned.

Sara began to go out sometimes with the wise woman. She learned to pick the herbs and make medicine. Even now, so soon after all the snow we had, there were some to be found. She went to people's houses and helped to cure their ills. I was apprehensive at first, but she came back at night. Miriam came to pick her up sometimes, it depended which direction she was going, and I went to extremes to make her feel welcome.

Now the rabbits were starting to become better fed, and though it took a while, they gradually became more abundant. I took some down to my friends at the tannery to fulfil my debts, and I chopped the trees down and made a pile of logs that would last them for some while.

They asked me about Sara.

"Oh, she is learning the trade of a wise woman. She knows about herbs and sometimes goes to make people well when they are sick."

"And how do you feel about it?"

"There's nothing I can do about it so I try to show that it's all right."

"Good, you are learning," Thomas said.

"Miriam says she will take her to a childbirth and let her help."

"What does she feel about that, with what happened to her mother?"

"She's all right about it. It wasn't her, it was me who blamed father." Thomas and Martha exchanged glances, but I knew how I felt. "He shouldn't have made us watch, and he should have got the wise woman straight away."

"I don't think you should say that to Sara."

"Father seemed to think, because it had worked out before, it would always be all right."

"But Sara didn't think that way, did she?"

"Miriam did, you should have seen her eyes. I think she put the evil eye on him and he never got over it."

Thomas put his arm across my shoulder. "Don't let it make you sour, or you will regret it."

"Oh, I know better than to say a thing to Sara now."

"Good," Martha said.

Life continued like this for the next year or two. We didn't set so many traps now. There was only Sara and me, and rabbits only had a lot of value if people were hungry, mainly at the end of the year. I used to fetch some fish nowadays, keeping carefully among the trees by the third and biggest pond. I usually got a fair catch.

I used to get the meals cooked if Sara had been out for a long day. She had been to several births, and Miriam said she was confident enough to leave her in charge sometimes. People used to come for her if they were ill now, if we were the nearest.

Martha and Thomas knew her; she had been looking after someone who lived near them. They were as impressed as everyone else seemed to be.

I was twelve now and Sara thirteen, but most people thought she was a good deal older. She had grown taller than me, and people respected her for her skills.

Martha once asked her if she had still got her coat.

"Oh yes," she said. "It is lovely to be able to keep myself warm in the cold weather. I never did thank you for it."

"That's all right, John did, and he came when the snow was at its worst. He really wanted to look after you."

"I know," Sara said. "But he shouldn't have, he made himself very sick. I thought I would lose him, but Miriam managed to save him."

"He's a good lad."

"Yes, I know, he does his best."

Miriam kept her promise and showed us just where our parents were buried, but her little name-board was long gone. We went inside the church and just sat in the quiet for what seemed a long time, just as the man in the strange flowing robes had said we should. I don't know what was supposed to have happened, but it was an odd, somehow calming, experience. I was glad Sara sat with me. It made us seem close again.

Just after this I got my first job, I became a brick-maker. They certainly needed lots of bricks for the new place they were building across the canal. It looked to me as if Ironville would be as big as Alfreton when it was finally done. All the houses were going to be of brick, not just anything that could be cobbled together. It would be a marvel to behold. I even heard that they intended to build a new church; we wouldn't have to go to Alfreton, that is to say, if we ever needed one.

Soon there would be people living in the houses, the people who worked in the pits, the forges, and the ironworks in Butterley.

For me, it was a long day and tedious work. But I thought, we shall have some money and they can't put us in that workhouse, which was nearing completion, along the Lea Lane in nearby Alfreton.

Sara just smiled when I told her why I was doing it.

The only thing was, I was becoming more like one of the zombies who still walked along the canal side every day, with just one difference, that I didn't have the black face.

I would come home each day and drop asleep across the bed. Sara had to wake me to eat my meals.

"This isn't necessary, you know," Sara said one day, when she woke me. "Just how much money do you think you need so that no one will cart you off to that place? It's a pity you can't see some of the places I go to, then you would know what it is to have nothing."

It didn't make us better off. We had always had everything we needed, plenty of food, a roof over our heads. So we hadn't got any money, but then we had never needed any.

Sara took to checking the traps again and making the food. And she still went out with Miriam when anyone was in need.

I had watched the builders making the houses and was sure when the opportunity came, I would be able to build myself a proper brick house, not just a cott for Sara and me. In my mind it was always Sara and me. I couldn't see anything coming between us ever.

Slowly the idea was forming in my mind. I would get a job as a builder. I could make bricks as well as any man on earth, now I would learn to make a house, then all I needed was a piece of land. What is more I should have the funds to buy the land.

I knew the builders, from them fetching their bricks, and I began to sound them out. Eventually I got my new job at Browns the builders.

Once I started doing my building job I didn't feel anything like so tired. Perhaps I was getting stronger with age, or then maybe it just wasn't so repetitious. Either way I felt comfortable and part of this brave new world.

We still lived in the cott. I hadn't seen Thomas and Martha for some time, but Sara kept them informed about what I was doing. I got her to promise that one of us would take them some rabbits when the seasons turned. After all, winter was the time when most people needed some extra food.

The next few years went by.

I still stocked up with wood on the Sundays.

The bargemen never went as far as the old wharf; in fact they had long ago made themselves another one, further down the canal, so that they could load the coal easier.

The barge that had caught fire had long ago been broken up and burnt, so that it didn't remind them of the dangers, but the water had still caught fire again sometimes. It was very strange.

From time to time we heard of parts of the common lands being fenced in, it was called 'the Enclosure Acts'. Normally it went to the big landowners, like the lords of the manors, who got the lion's share. But sometimes some small plots went to ordinary folks like us.

I tried to find out, through Henry Brown the builder, or Thomas and Martha. I asked Miriam if she knew how anyone got a piece of common land. It seemed a big mystery. Either no one knew, or they didn't want to tell me.

I thought even an area like Ironville, where it seemed as if they were building this whole big town, had been common land, so how had they done it? Of course, I hadn't the chance to talk to the big men.

How had someone been able to pinch our brook and build a canal that stretched for miles across what had always been common land? My mind was full of all these things, and I now knew that it had been built by a boy called Benjamin Outram, who was in his mid thirties, and so not a lot older than I was.

I had no idea of how anyone could get a piece of common land. I asked everyone I could, but it seemed a total secret.

Chapter 5

The Reverend Henry Case who had married the widow of George Morewood, he who had been the Lord of the Manor of Alfreton, lived in isolated splendour in Alfreton Hall.

Now the man of the cloth took ill and, because he had no more faith in the medical profession than most of his time, he sent for the wise woman. Miriam duly arrived with her assistant Sara, who gazed with sheer astonishment at the splendour of the hall. They were shown to the bedroom and found the inmate totally covered in sweat, and bemoaning his condition.

Sara immediately said to Miriam, "It's no more than an aggie bout, he will be better in about four days, with or without any treatment."

Miriam silenced her with a look then turned to the woman who had led her to the sickroom.

"Get a bowl of warm water and rinse him down, then get some fresh sheets on the bed. Oh, and some flowers in a vase to make the place more cheerful, then you can open a window to allow some air to come into the room. I'll come tomorrow and he should be a lot better."

"I'll get a maid."

The wise woman fixed her big dark eyes on her and the woman fled.

Miriam put some powder she had made earlier into a cup of warm water and putting an arm behind his back she lifted him up. Then she held his head forward and put the drink to his lips, encouraging him to drink. He drank it, spluttered a little, and lay back onto the pillow.

Miriam now sat on a chair beside his bed and took hold of the man's hand. She spoke softly into his ear, "They will come and clean you up. Stay in bed all today, you should go to sleep as soon as they are done, tomorrow we will come back. All being well, we will get you up into this chair, I think you will soon be all right."

The man's rasping, croaky voice said something that Sara didn't hear, but Miriam just smiled.

The woman who had shown Sara and Miriam to the room now came back with two other women, one of whom was carrying the bowl and a sponge. The wise woman directed them what to do, and they carried out their duties efficiently, and left at a nod from the lady of the house.

The Reverend Henry Case settled back and went to sleep.

"Will he be all right?"

"That is in the hands of the Almighty, but I would expect him to be up and about in two or three days," Miriam said, and added, "I would also expect him to sleep for about the next twenty-four hours, then I will see him again."

Mrs Case showed them the way along the corridors, down some stairs and into the late afternoon sunlight. It was only as they left the mansion that Mrs Case spoke and then it was little more than, "Thank you for coming."

We still lived without the need of the money I brought home and carefully hid in a hole covered with reeds. Totally undetectable, without someone informing of its whereabouts.

I had almost given up hope of getting a piece of enclosed common land large enough to build my house, a real house made of bricks not a cott, for Sara and me.

Sara told me of the abject poverty that was the lot of many of the people that they visited. I was almost at the point of giving away the useless money stored so carefully in its little safe.

Sara did take a rabbit or two sometimes, that would serve to nourish some of the worst cases, saying. "It's not herbs or money a lot of them need, it's food," and indeed some speedy recoveries proved her point.

It had rained heavily the previous day, and through the night and Henry Brown had told us not to bother coming unless the weather broke, we wouldn't be able to do a lot of building. So I was still around when Miriam called to fetch Sara.

She raised her eyes inquiringly when she saw me. So I answered her unspoken inquiry with the words, "Bad weather, we can't build much in this lot."

She nodded wordlessly.

Sara had put her coat on, more as a something to keep her dry than warm, and they set off.

As Miriam had forecast the previous day, the new Lord of the Manor was already looking far better than he had done the previous day. He was already sitting up on his chair. He had thick bushy eyebrows and a magnificent moustache that somehow didn't sit well beneath a completely bald head. And he had a twinkle in his eye that hadn't been there yesterday.

It was Sara who spoke first, unaware of the protocol of waiting to be spoken to by someone of his position.

"It's nice to see you looking a little better than when we last saw you sir."

The eyes of the lady of the house fixed on her, but the invalid calmed what could have been an awkward moment. "It is thanks to you good ladies for my wellbeing."

Miriam walked to the bed and took hold of his wrist, then put her hand across his forehead. "The fever seems to have broken sir, I think you will be all right now."

"You have my eternal gratitude, I had visions of some quack bleeding me with those disgusting leeches. Name your fee, I will see it is discharged in full."

"I don't think there is anything we need from you, not at this time sir," Miriam said. She turned and began to walk towards the door, stopped, and turned back towards the man sitting beside his bed. "I don't know if this is within your remit sir."

"Just ask."

She stood there, as if wondering just how to express her request.

"When the next lot of common land is up for enclosure, would it be possible for a consideration of a small piece to be allotted to Sara's brother. He has always dreamt of building his own house."

"Impossible!" the Lady of the Manor almost screamed.

"That is all right madam, I hope you don't mind my enquiry," Miriam replied in her most deferential voice.

The two women walked towards the door.

"I think we can find our own way out."

It was the invalid who spoke next.

"I don't know how the procedure works, but I will certainly enquire for you."

"Thank you sir".

As they made their way through the maze of passages and down the stairway Miriam whispered softly, "Give it time, but I think John will get his piece of land, and make his house. Just tell him to be patient."

During the next few days Sara was unusually quiet. Miriam spotted it first, I was full of my own problems. I was trying to get as much money as I could. I needed it to get as many bricks as possible when my allotment of common land came up.

Miriam warned me, "Don't get your hopes too high, it might be years, it could be never."

"I know, I may have to wait until he is ill again, Sara told me, but sooner or later he will need you and Sara, then he will remember."

"People like that don't always remember their obligations."

"It's not only people like that, people in general only think of what is best for themselves."

Miriam smiled. "Oh John, you have got a cynical attitude towards the human race. If you are like that at fourteen, just what will you be like when you are grown, a bitter twisted old man?"

"I was just saying what everyone else says."

"And just who do you go and talk with?"

"Only Mr Brown the builder."

It was quiet for a while. It was then that I said, "I will get it one day, you know, for Sara and me."

Miriam seemed thoughtful. "Maybe that is it, Sara and you."

"What."

"Well you always talk as if you are married, together for ever. Sara might have her own plans."

"What plans?"

"Well she is growing into a lady, she might want a man of her own."

"We have always been together."

"And you still sleep in the same bed, don't you? Perhaps she is starting to get embarrassed, and not wanting to be in the same bed as her brother."

"I wouldn't do anything to embarrass Sara."

"Perhaps it's not your fault, it's just nature's work."

"What shall I do?"

"If that's it, I don't think there is anything you can do."

"Is that what Sara has been telling you?"

"No, she hasn't said a single word, but girls grow up, and boys too, they need to explore, with other girls and boys."

"Sara knows what happened to her mother, she wouldn't do things like that."

"How many girls do you know who live with their brothers? Or the other way round. It just doesn't happen like that."

"I don't know any other people, just me and Sara. We are not like other people anyway."

"I think sooner or later you will find that you are, both of you."

"I knew it was wrong her being with you all the time, she will learn those things."

"John, whatever you think now, I am only trying to warn you. And I am not just Sara's friend, but your friend as well."

"Do you really think anything will come of asking the squire about the land?"

"Often things happen later, I have just sowed a seed in his head, when he hears someone mention a land enclosure act he will remember."

"Henry Brown said this squire doesn't live in the Hall now, he lives at a church in Warwickshire, wherever that is."

"I wouldn't talk to Mr Brown, or anyone else about it, just wait and it will happen sooner or later."

"But you don't think Sara will come?"

"I don't know, she hasn't said a thing. It's just that I am a little bit older than you and I know a little bit more about the world."

"Oh," I said.

"Don't worry, everything will work out, and Sara will always be the best pal you ever have, and me as well, if you let me."

I hadn't thought about Miriam as a friend, she was always something different like, well, the wise woman. I suppose that now Sara was becoming something of a wise woman too, but I couldn't look on Sara as something different.

After I had reflected like that for a while I said, "Thank you Miriam, I will like that." Then I added, "I suppose you have been a good friend already. You got me better when I was in a mess, and you didn't have any payment from the squire when you could have asked for something big."

"I'll let you know something, you can get a lot more from those sort of people by not asking, sometimes."

"Or they go off to Warwickshire and forget altogether."

"It's a chance you take in life."

Sara, who had been outside, now came back in. "Just what have you two been talking about so earnestly?"

"Oh, just not to get my hope's up too quickly, and other bits and bobs."

Nothing on Miriam's face gave away any emotion.

She turned to Sara. "I want you to be the one to see to Mrs Beastal now, do you think you can do it?"

"Yes of course, but I would have thought she was the most important person right now."

"She is, that is why I want you to do it."

"Will you be there when the baby comes?"

"Not unless you think you need me."

I lifted my ears at this. "Baby, can you do that Sara?"

"Yes." Her answer was strong and confident.

"But mother?"

"I could have done that as well, if I had known what I know now."

Miriam smiled, how much did I really know my sister.

The women left.

I sat on the bed and suddenly I felt distinctly odd, my stomach was churning. Sara was going to see a woman who was doing what mother had been doing in the dirt on the floor of our cott.

Was Miriam doing this to remind her of all the pain and degradation she could suffer if she went off with a man, so that she would never do anything like it? But Sara wasn't frightened at all. In fact, she looked positively glowing as she had left me alone, just sitting on the bed.

Sara didn't come back that night, or the next. In fact it was midway through the third day when she finally arrived home. She was tired but very happy.

"I did it, it's a baby girl. They say they will call her Sara after me."

"Didn't Miriam come?"

"No, you heard her say I could do it."

"But three days, it must have been terrible."

"No, it was wonderful, now I'm tired."

She flopped over the bad.

I asked her if she wanted anything, but she was already asleep, so I just pulled the coat across her and stood wondering at this little sister of mine.

Sara slept for about twelve hours, a blissfully 'unaware of the world' type of sleep, and woke just after Miriam had arrived. Maybe it was the sound of Miriam's voice that disturbed her. I hadn't gone to do my building work, Mr Brown was tolerant of my absenteeism. It didn't happen often, and he said I worked harder than the others anyway.

I was just telling Miriam that it had been unfair to expect Sara to undergo the ordeal she had, especially after what had happened to her mother, when she awoke and raised herself on one elbow.

"Thank you Miriam." Her voice interrupted my complaints.

"How was it?" Miriam asked.

"Wonderful. I had to turn the baby, but I did it. I'm so grateful for your confidence in me."

I could hardly believe my ears, Sara talking like that, so confident when she knew everything that might have happened.

I said, "But you are only fifteen."

"I think you will find she is a woman, not a child any more John. I warned you these things happen, and it doesn't matter if she is fifteen or thirty."

"I could never do anything like that."

"You have believed you are the grown-up, running the whole thing, and you are fourteen, but I am afraid Sara can do everything you can. I'm sorry John, but she has had to grow up, just as much as you have, maybe more."

"You didn't have to let her do this though."

"But you see I did, I had to know, and Sara had to know too."

I looked at Sara's face simply radiating vitality.

"Oh," I said, standing there, unable to completely understand my new position in the great scheme of things. It was as if the bottom had fallen out of my whole world. I didn't matter any more.

I didn't need to make bricks. I didn't need to make houses. I no longer believed Sara would want to live in my/our new house, and without Sara what was the point? There didn't seem to be any pressure on leaving the cott. Did I even want my piece of enclosed common land?

Miriam had walked over to talk to Sara. I just slipped out into the strangely empty afternoon. I don't know how long it was before either of them had even noticed.

There was a time when I would have gone to talk to my friends at the tannery but I didn't even want to tell them how everything had changed. I didn't want to go back to building houses for Henry Brown, nothing I could ever do could compare with what my sister had done, and I knew it.

I carried on working at my building job, outwardly everything was the same. I hadn't seen my friends at the tannery for months, when one day Sara announced that she was going to see Mrs Roberts. The name meant nothing to me until she added, "At the tannery."

"Tannery, you mean Martha, what's wrong?"

"Nothing, she's nearing her time, that's all."

"Time, you mean baby? I didn't know, why didn't you tell me?"

"She asked me not to, she knows how you feel about babies."

I found out that Miriam had been trying to help her conceive for a while now.

So it came to pass that Martha Roberts bore her first child, and named him Samuel. He was the first of many, and she also called one later on Sara, and another John. "In honour of two good friends."

General historical notes to evaluate the story

At the time of John Barlow's birth, there were no religious establishments within the parish of Alfreton other than St Martin's, the ancient parish church. It was indeed an irreligious, lawless place.

Towards the end of the eighteenth century when the tall, august John Wesley, the great hell-fire spiritual reformer, visited the area, dressed entirely in black and riding a great black horse, there began a spiritual revival. A great number of churches and chapels were built in Alfreton and in the surrounding hamlets, and indeed throughout the land, beginning just after the death of Wesley, as an old man approaching his nineties, in 1796. So it was that in John Barlow's lifetime he would witness not only great industrial changes, but religious changes as well.

John mentions the new *George Hotel* at the crest of the hill approaching Alfreton church. In fact there were many coaching inns, public houses and alehouses in both the main town and suburbs. *The Angel* in King Street was mentioned as early as 1553, and there were many others almost as old. Water wasn't considered a very safe drink generally and ale was the drink of the majority. Alcoholism was rife, even in children. The open sewers that flowed both down the centre of King Street, and some 200 yards further east, joined together to flow down from the crest of the hill to the almost stagnant pond known as the horse-wash. At the time of the building of the turnpike roads in the early 1800s by mainly Irish labourers, the conditions were so bad that many, not having the immune system built up by the locals, succumbed to diseases like cholera, typhoid etc. caused by the local conditions. Indeed the average life expectancy at that time in the area was only thirty-seven years, making it comparable with London's East End as the worst place to live in the country.

Summer-cotts, the place where the shepherds had their windbreaks, now became a hamlet and, as it gradually extended up the hill, becoming the village of Somercotes.

It is known that John had his enclosure of 400 square yards on Somercotes common at the time of his death in the year 1844, which would have been in his 44th year. Although when he actually acquired it is not known. Had he just acquired it, or could he conceivably have had it and done nothing with it for twenty years or more, other than just putting a pile of bricks on it and then using it as no more than a spot to tether his goat?

It is open to conjecture if John or Sara married, if they were together still, or indeed if Sara was alive in that year.

The strange case of what happened to the younger brothers and sisters was never again mentioned.

Another historical fact was that Somercotes common was already enclosed by the year 1811, and that the squire, the Reverend Henry Case Morewood, had the lion's share of the common land. However, the piece of ground that John obtained appears to have come, not from the squire, but an isolated piece of common land that had never been allocated adjoining the lands of a Mr Dawes another landowner.

In other nearby villages, including Selston, the common wasn't enclosed until the year 1890. None of this seems satisfactorily explained.

John didn't seem aware of the fact that if a building had a roof and was in general occupation, during his tenure of the cott, then he should have been allowed to remain in his dwelling. Anyhow, it seems almost inconceivable that no one was aware of the family living in the edge of the woods, between Riddings and the canal at Ironville for a good many years.

As mentioned, the oil rig in the Riddings was up and going by the year 1847, three years after John's death, and yielding up to 300 gallons a day of a substance known as naphtha. Later, this became more cloudy and was then described as paraffin.

A special meeting was organized with the Royal Society in which Dr Young demonstrated his petroleum to the noted scientist Sir Humphry Davy.

Gas was also found, but it was very deep underground, and at the time the technology didn't exist to extract it. Perhaps some time in the future someone will find out if this is in large enough quantities to be of commercial value.

The Two Josephs' Story

The Reverend William Howard, vicar of St Martin's church in Alfreton, had conducted the burial service for John Barlow in May 1844 and, true to his promise, had contacted the two Josephs.

Joseph Carlin and Joseph Rhodes were speculators, even though both were only in their early to mid twenties. They wanted to know of anyone who had died with any property and seemingly no near relatives, and they paid handsomely for any information about property that might become available.

Nominally, Joseph Carlin was a baker and Joseph Rhodes an engineer, but they had their eyes and ears to the ground for any quick money that was to be had. And any knowledge was their stock-in-trade.

So it was that the two Josephs had visited the reclaimed former common land and been surprised to find the neat stacks of bricks and a tethered goat, munching at the still available grass with no idea of the trauma that had occurred.

Common land wasn't the main value, but a ready supply of bricks, neatly stacked and waiting for development, this was more interesting.

Who was the actual owner now that John Barlow was no more?

The vicar had said he knew of no relatives, but someone must have paid for the interment. Some more inquiries had to be made, but none too intrusive if they were to acquire the land, and the handy supply of bricks.

Joseph Carlin was particularly keen. This place was ideally situated along the main track, called the Greenhill Lane, now joining onto the just opened Nottingham/Alfreton toll road. And the locality was developing quickly, what with the coal mines, the iron ore deposits, the canal not far away, and the new toll roads which were radiating from Alfreton throughout the whole area. And then Mr Stevenson's railways were also adding to the development, coming straight across the region.

Not only that, there was now this new stuff called oil they said would be coming from the ground a little further along the Greenhill Lane, in the next village now called Riddings. They were already building a strange thing called a derrick, from which this stuff would squirt from the ground. Although the two Josephs never pretended they understood what it was, or how it could be used, they were deeply conscious that any new development would mean more people, and therefore more money into the area.

The heap of bricks neatly stacked on four hundred square yards of fenced former common land, was a fascination to the two Josephs. They could make a bakery, a dairy parlour, or almost anything with the pile of bricks already there and waiting, and he, Joseph Carlin, could run it.

They would have to tread carefully, but the opportunity was there. If the business didn't come off, then they could sell it as a going concern and move on.

Joseph Rhodes as an engineer, could draw up the plans, but first he had to discover if there were any close relatives, cousins didn't count. Before anyone could find out what was happening, the whole place would be up and running.

Once a place was built, and there was occupation, who was to say that an agreement hadn't been formally made between the parties. An official-looking document could be produced, it had happened before many times.

The two Josephs were no better, or worse, than the average of their day. They had acquired their money, a bit here and a bit there, by many such scams. Usually they were long gone before any arguments tested the validity of their dealings, but in truth, no irate clients had ever pursued them. This, however, was something different. Joseph Carlin was aiming to test the theory to its bitter end. He intended to be the one who was living in the development. He would face the relatives, if there were any, or the authorities if it came to that.

Joseph Rhodes was dubious; he still preferred to be long gone.

Another enquiry to the vicar revealed that the funeral had been paid for from some unknown source, all very mysterious. But would this unknown source try to claim the land? Well the Reverend Howard didn't seem to think so, perhaps he knew more than he was saying.

They did find out from the vicar that John Barlow had been living in Ironville, which was the new development being built for the Butterley Company. An inquiry revealed that no one seemed to know the name of John Barlow at the Butterley works, nor in the new village. How could anyone be so anonymous?

How had anyone obtained the property? To get a piece of common land he had to have had some contacts at least, and this man had also presumably bought enough bricks to build something substantial.

Anyone living in the new village must work within the company, yet no one seemed to have any knowledge of him at all.

Joseph Carlin resolved to dig a foundation trench and lay a course of bricks along the south side of the property, then wait a while for any protests. If within a week or two nothing happened they would produce a convincing document and after that it would be all systems go. The house would be first then once they were resident on the land well, possession is nine-tenths of the law. What they would have been doing was no different to what they had done before.

Joseph Rhodes wanted nothing to do with such a risky enterprise. He would have been happy to have commandeered the land and sold it to someone else who could have done whatever they wanted, providing the two Josephs were long gone. What he didn't want was to be the ones to have to answer any awkward questions, should that situation occur. He intended to distance himself from this one, as they had always done, but to his friend the opportunity was too good to resist.

Chapter 2

It was Joseph Carlin alone who made the trip to *Obadiah Watkins, Smith and Belton*, the long-established solicitors whose premises dominated Main Street in Heanor town.

Joseph asked to see Mr Smith.

"He has someone with him at present, will someone else do?" the girl replied.

"No, I usually see Mr Smith. Will he be long or shall I come back?" he asked.

"I don't think he will be long, who shall I say wants to see him?"

"Joseph Carlin."

The girl gave no indication that she had even heard his reply, and carried on shuffling the same papers she had been arranging when he had come in.

Joseph sat down and waited. Some ten minutes later a man emerged and the girl got up and went into the lawyer's office.

Ben Smith soon appeared at the door. He was a big, heavily-built man of about forty-five years of age with a strikingly high forehead, topped with an almost completely hairless head.

"Joseph." He extended a great bear-like paw that served as a hand.

Joseph had forgotten the strength in that hand and he tried not to show the very real pain that he felt.

"Where is the other Joseph?" he asked. "No rifts in paradise, I hope?"

"No, nothing like that, it's just that I am doing this thing on my own."

Joseph explained about this piece of reclaimed land on Somercotes Common, along the Greenhill track.

"You are sure no one else is laying a claim to it then?"

"There is no one."

"I always thought you liked to do it together and move on as quickly as possible."

"Not this time, I want to set up a bakery of my own."

Ben Smith, after a little fumbling in some drawers and shuffling of papers, eventually withdrew a mass of documents from a sheath.

"Oh, it's now called Leabrooks Road along that part, they have altered a lot of the street names round there. Lea lane is now Sleetmoor Lane."

He was talking more to himself than to Joseph, as he riffled through the papers. Finally he withdrew a single map.

"Somercotes Common. Oh, that was already enclosed by the year 1811 so someone else must already have owned it."

The lawyer was still talking almost to himself.

"Yes," Joseph agreed. "That someone was John Barlow."

Joseph was used to his ruminating so he waited for the lawyer to continue. Eventually Ben Smith said, "If there is no one else to claim the holding you are perfectly at liberty to stake your claim, as it were."

"And if I happened to be in possession of a deed to say that John Barlow had passed it to me, then that ensures the legality."

"Yes, of course, but only if no one can produce another witnessed transferral."

"Subject to those provisions you will be able to give me the necessary papers?"

"Do you want the deeds dating from today?"

"Hardly, Mr Barlow died in May."

"He agreed to the transfer before then, did he?"

"Yes."

"All right, in that case I had better put March on the transfer."

"I think that would be perfect".

So Joseph Carlin had the deeds in his own name, dated the fifteenth day of March 1844, duly authorised by *Obadiah Watkins, Smith and Belton*, and signed by Mr Ben Smith.

The foundations were dug and a low-lying wall soon appeared along the south perimeter. Joseph Carlin waited most of the rest of the year of 1844. He was cautious, still waiting to see who would contest the validity of his tenuous claim. His erstwhile partner had made it quite clear that he was totally on his own. He was long gone.

Feeling gradually more confident, and with a legal document safely in his possession, he was often to be seen around the area during the month of November and early December, and no one questioned his right.

The December weather was mild and suddenly the development began to get under way. Two builders began to build on the low wall, it grew quickly and within a matter of weeks, to a trained eye, there was definitely the outline of a shop, with a bakery just behind it. It extended backwards along the southern boundary into an extensive living quarter, indicating a man of some substance. Joseph Carlin knew that the more impressive the development, the less likely that the average man would ask questions.

There was still few people around anyway; an old farmstead opposite, a stone cottage a little further along. Their owners appeared to be uninterested types, but the road seemed to be well repaired, and more and more people appeared to be using it. No one ever enquired as to what he was doing and what right he had to do it.

Joseph Carlin was soon resident in his comfortable home. He had never felt more at ease in anything he had ever done than he felt now. Joseph Rhodes visited him one day. He appeared more nervous than his friend, who showed him his new ovens and told him of his plans to begin production of bread. He intended to build stables for at least three horses behind the house covering the whole of the eastern perimeter. "I shall then be able to deliver my bread to anyone who wants to buy it."

"That is the whole point, every housewife makes her own bread, who is going to buy it?"

"There will always be some who will buy, people who want to seem that little bit better than their neighbours. They will want everyone seeing the brand new horse and dray outside their house, and I will soon have my dairy up and running as well, with butter and cheese."

Joseph Rhodes was still dubious.

"This isn't what we do, we let others take the risks, we take our cut and then we are long gone."

"Look, I have been round to see how some of the people have fared on the lands we have got them. There hasn't been a single comeback anywhere. Some are doing very well."

"And some have failed completely."

"Look, I will be with you on any new venture, we will still be partners."

"No we won't, you will be spending every minute trying to ensure this place doesn't fail, and it doesn't even have to be your fault, anything can happen."

"It will be all right."

"We shall see."

Joseph Rhodes extended his hand and his friend took it.

"I really do wish you the very best of luck."

"Goodbye."

"Keep in touch."

The friends parted.

Chapter 3

Larry Jackson was a man of about thirty-five years of age. He had been making bread all his working life and now he had come to see Joseph with a view to being his baker. His credentials were impeccable, his having done a similar job in Sheffield.

"Why have you come away from a place like that to try to find work in the wilds?"

"Well sir, my wife's parents live locally, and they have both been sick for months. She has come to tend them in their final illnesses. I have a Sunday off so I came to see just what is happening, and when she is likely to return home."

"Just take her back then, she belongs to you now not them."

"Yes I could do that, but they have a fine house, and if I could find work here I'd have a nicer place to live, and everyone would be better off."

"So when they die you will be off again."

"No sir, I thought that if you would give me a chance to prove myself, I would like to settle in the area."

"And live in a fine house, into the bargain?"

"Yes, it could work out very well all round."

Joseph Carlin gave Larry the tour, asked him if he was used to the type of ovens he had installed, and was given the reassurance that they were the very same as those he had used for the last few years. Joseph explained just where he intended to build his dairy next to the bakery and shop, with a passage in between so that the horses could get between the buildings to the stables behind the main development, along the eastern boundary so that the whole lot would be an enclosed square. And if he put a gateway across the top everything would be fully private.

"It will be a fine place sir, I'd venture to say one of the very best in the whole county."

Larry doffed his cap as he spoke, in the same way as he would to gentry. Joseph allowed himself a smile. He really was on his way up.

The two men parted, Joseph assuring him that it would be only a case of buying a suitable horse and dray, and getting a supply of ingredients like flour etc. He expected to begin with a trial run in a little over a week.

The clement weather, which had helped the work come along so well, couldn't be expected to last for ever, nor could the extreme good fortune that Joseph had enjoyed.

He had been sitting comfortably beside the wood fire watching the flames dancing in the hearth. In his mind he contemplated if it wouldn't be the ideal time to take a wife. He would certainly need someone to cook and clean, it would be cheaper than having a cleaner to do the work, and they had their other uses to. He didn't even think of love, just the advantages of the union.

Most women found him personable, and now his prospects were considerably enhanced, he would soon be an employer. Larry Jackson had doffed his cap in respect to his position. Joseph smiled at his thoughts. Joseph Rhodes would soon regret losing his opportunity to be part of this latest adventure.

He stood up and opened the door to get some more logs to dry out in the warm of the room. He was in for a surprise. It had been cold lately, but now the temperature had warmed to the extent that he believed there wouldn't be any snow this winter. But he had been wrong. It was snowing hard. The ground was already covered in a sea of unbroken whiteness, all in a matter of a couple of hours since he had closed out the elements. Bringing in the logs was the sort of job a wife would have done. He shivered at the unexpected cold, or maybe at the psychological effects of seeing the snow. He closed the door and settled once more in front of the hearth. He wouldn't be opening it again that night.

Chapter 4

John Henry Lawence, High Sheriff and chief magistrate for the county of Derbyshire, accepted a bottle of the finest port wine from his guest and shook his hand. He knew the portly figure of Job Dawes, a local landowner, well enough to realise that this unexpected visit wasn't purely social.

"Now Job, just what would make you choose to come, bringing me a bottle of your very best port wine, when you could be enjoying the company of some blonde bimbo in the local tavern?"

"John Henry, you do me an injustice."

The tall, distinguished-looking High Sheriff had put the bottle down on the table and was waiting for some sort of explanation.

Unlike the lawyer, Job liked to take his time in broaching any subject.

"I thought it would be better to come and have an informal talk to an old friend, sooner than come to your office. This is friendlier, more casual, if you see what I mean."

"What you really mean is that instead of a consultation fee, you could bring me a bottle of wine."

"John Henry, you know I like to call on you from time to time."

"When you want something."

"I think we are getting off on the wrong foot. I have been sorely wronged and I called on a friend for advice."

"Go on."

"Well, someone is squatting on my land, not only that, but they are building houses and moving in, that can't be legal."

"And you are the legal owner?"

"Of course."

"Just where is this land?"

"It's along the old Greenhill track in Somercotes, they call it Leabrooks Road now."

"I assume you can prove ownership."

"Of course, my father got it more than thirty years ago in the fencing of the common land."

"You want me to look into it then?"

"I want you to jail the criminals, they should be hung."

"All right, I'll look into it then. Drop me the papers in to prove your ownership."

"Thank you John Henry, you are a true friend." He extended a hand, which the lawyer took reluctantly.

"All I said is that I will look into it. But whatever I find I shall report it as it is, no favours, just the truth."

It was a pig of a night and the wind was howling outside as Joseph Carlin slipped into his bed. The covers were cold and he gave an involuntary shudder and pulled them closer. If he had a wife he could let her warm them before he got in. He smiled at the thought. Today was the first time he had considered himself anything but fancy free in the pursuance of his fortune. He would need kids to follow him, kids to work in his bakery.

A wife would have to bring a dowry with her, of course, he couldn't be expected to keep her. The more he mulled it over in his mind the more attractive the prospect became. And connections with local dignitaries would enhance his standing locally. If she was pretty, so much the better, but mainly she had to be rich.

Tomorrow he would go and see a miller, there were several in and around Somercotes. One along Sleetmoor Lane had taken his fancy. It looked to be a new development, painted white and gleaming in the sunlight when he had first seen it. It must be someone go-ahead like himself, they could do each other a lot of good. He would check that his prices were competitive of course, then it would be all systems go. He smiled to himself. Soon he would need a lot of horses and drays.

Both of the two Josephs had always let their imaginations run riot. But this time he was going alone, he would show the other Joseph just what a mistake he had made.

Soon he felt relaxed, warm and totally content and he drifted into a sound, dreamless sleep without a care in the whole world.

The next morning he put some small sticks on the embers of last night's fire and raked the ashes from under the grate. As it kindled he added logs, then some turf to ensure it didn't burn away too quickly. Now, after putting on some warm garments, he was ready to explore the world outside. The snow wasn't as bad as he had expected.

Purposefully he set out to see the miller, striding out up the road and turning left on to Sleetmoor Lane. He walked along the lane, past the great fortress of a building on the left-hand side and thought for a minute that it must be a prison. When he saw the little plaque that read *The Workhouse* he gave it a last inquisitive glance then carried on until he reached the post-mill at the far end of the lane.

It had been constructed on an oak tree stump, about three feet in diameter, with heavy oak crosspieces to take the weight of a three-storey structure which could be turned by hand to face the wind so that the sails would turn and grind the corn. Joseph stood looking at the building, suitably impressed.

Confidently he asked for the master and was taken to see Mr John Marples the miller, who he had expected to be a young man like himself just starting out on his career. But the miller was well into his forties, in an age when life expectancy was little more than that. The man was fat, bald and jovial, seemingly without a care in the world. He extended a podgy hand and revealed a firm grip.

"What can I do for you, young man?"

"My name is Joseph Carlin. May I first congratulate you on the fine building you have here sir?"

"Yes, we have made a good job of doing the place up since I took over from old Hardy."

"Well," Joseph began, "the fact is, I am starting a bakery along Leabrooks Road and I will be needing a supplier of flour, and any advice I can get."

"John Marples at your service, maker of the finest flour in the area."

"How long have you been in the trade sir?"

"Almost thirty-five years, man and boy."

"I thought your mill looked new," Joseph said.

"Totally refurbished, new machinery, need to keep up with modern ideas you know."

"If you don't mind me asking, have you sons to follow you in the trade?"

"No, just a daughter, but as good as any son could have possibly been."

"Yes but… " Joseph began, thought better of it, and stopped.

"She had her mind on the business as well as any boy could do."

Joseph deftly changed the subject.

"I was interested in your prices, as well as the quality."

"I think you will find us as competitive as anyone. I'll give you a couple of bags and let you judge for yourself lad. Then we will talk prices."

"Well I can't ask for anything better than that."

Joseph Carlin liked this jolly miller.

Unbeknown to Joseph Carlin, another conversation was taking place not a mile from where he now stood. A conversation that, had he been privy to it, would have alarmed him greatly.

George Rhodes, tall, gaunt, slightly stooped, father of his friend Joseph, was running his hand through his thinning hair, as he was speaking to the more rotund, red-faced Job Dawes, former owner of the land on which the new bakery now stood. The senior Mr Rhodes had never liked the friendship between the two Josephs and now saw a chance to usurp the premises, and at the same time break up the pair for good.

He had conducted the occasional business deal with his fellow farmer Mr Dawes, and they had been on speaking terms for a good few years. Now he brought over a drink of the *George Hotel's* finest beer and passed it to the other man. It had been market day and both had been at Alfreton market, buying some young calves for fattening. George had deferred to his friend in the bidding to allow Job the chance of a nice little bargain with one set of calves, so it was no great surprise when the drink came over.

"I thought there was something you were wanting, I was just trying to think what it could possibly be."

"Why Job, you do me an injustice, I was just helping an old friend."

In no way deceived, Job Dawes waited for his fellow farmer to continue, while looking him steadily in the eye.

"It was just that I wondered why you let a prime piece of land bordering the main street go to a speculator like young Carlin."

"Wasn't my land, I'd let it go a long while ago, as a sort of favour to John Barlow."

There was no way Job Dawes was going to tell a man like George Rhodes of his talk with the High Sheriff.

"That doesn't seem much like the hard-nosed Job Dawes I know," George continued.

"Proves you don't know as much about me as you think you do."

"But how has Carlin got hold of it?"

"Seems that John Barlow has died, so it's passed to him, nothing I can do."

"I wonder?" said George, a malevolent grin crossing his face. "See the thing is, I know a little about this Carlin, he's a bad sort."

"As I said, nothing to do with me."

"If Carlin doesn't own the site, then it automatically returns to you."

"I don't know, maybe, I suppose."

"I would make you an offer, a reasonable fee for the place as it stands."

"You don't know about bakeries, stick to farming, that's my advice."

"I don't know, but I know a man who does and I've got that man lined up."

"George, I won't do anything wrong, but if I get ownership I don't mind a little profit."

"We'll leave it at that for now then."

Job Dawes watched the other man leave the pub, he didn't particularly like the man but now, as another local man Henry Johnson spoke to him, he forgot about his dealings with Rhodes.

"Got a good deal with the calves Job."

"Yes," he agreed, his mind elsewhere. He finished his drink and left the pub, he still had to get the beasts back to the farm.

Things were beginning to move in his direction. With a little help from the High Sheriff he could soon have the land back in his possession, and if Rhodes really wanted to buy it, he wasn't averse to a quick profit.

George Rhodes wasn't ready to hurry home yet. After leaving the *George Hotel* he had walked a little way down the hill and entered the *Angel*. A smaller man was already waiting for him, he ordered two drinks, and joined the other man who had moved away from the bar and was seated alone at a table at the back of the room.

"Larry, what have you got to report?"

Larry Jackson sipped at his drink. It was the farmer who had recruited and paid him to get work from Joseph Carlin. Rhodes had told him he would have employment whatever happened so he gladly reported back that Carlin had visited a miller and was hoping to start a trial run of bread the following week.

"Is he now? I wonder what we can do to speed up the normal processes of the law?" He was talking almost to himself rather than to his companion.

He wasn't on close terms with the High Sheriff, but perhaps another word with Job Dawes wouldn't come amiss.

He slipped Larry his weekly payment and prepared to go.

"I'll see you next week, before if there are any developments."

Just behind the house and bakery, workmen were drilling for a well. It would be necessary to have a store of water to make his bread, but it was proving a bit more troublesome than he had thought. They had gone down some twenty feet before they struck water, then they had to plug it off before building a circular chamber, so that the water remained clean. They made a good job of it, and Joseph gave a mug of the pure liquid to a young lad who happened to be hanging around. It didn't seem to have done him any harm, so in his own mind he could pronounce it clean and he put a cover over it. So now another obstacle was taken out of the equation and he was in a position to begin production.

Joseph Carlin was wondering if it would be better to carry on with the building of the dairy, and so have the butter and cheese available to sell at the same time as his bread. But the sooner some money was coming back the better, up to now it had been all spending. His mind drifted back to the miller, or more towards his daughter. He hadn't met her, but a girl with her mind and eye on business... And surely the miller was wealthy enough and would provide a reasonable dowry. Everything was falling into place.

Perhaps if he didn't start soon he would lose his baker. After all the man would soon have to be earning something or he might go back to Sheffield.

The following week he would be making his trial run then, if he didn't start straight away, perhaps it would be better to put his baker on a retainer wage, enough so that he could live on it and would be prepared to wait a couple of weeks. The last thing he wanted was the man running back to Sheffield.

Larry mixed up a small dough and put it to one side, keeping it as warm as he could. Then some twelve hours later he mixed up another larger run and put some of the first, or sour dough, into it. This, when worked in well, provided the aeration necessary to make the dough rise, otherwise it couldn't rise and was an unleavened dough.

Larry obviously knew his trade. The loaves were a credit to the bakery, and to the flour that had been used in their manufacture.

Joseph gave most of it away to create the necessary good will. Ironically, one of the recipients of the first batch was the local farmer Job Dawes, whose wife had pronounced it one of the finest loaves she had tasted.

Another was the High Sheriff, whose household staff were equally loud in its praise, though their motives were a little different. If the sheriff's family liked it enough then that was one job they could dispense with. The only reason George Rhodes didn't get one was that his location was a little beyond the area that Joseph wished to travel.

However, the generosity of the gift only served to galvanise the sheriff. He had checked and had gained some surprising information about the ownership of the land. And he had given a lot of thought to his conversation with Job Dawes, and another meeting with George Rhodes. In the past, many the scam that seemed dubious he had let pass, because it had always seemed one man's word against another's. And these things seemed to drag on, and he finally had to make up his mind one way or the other when he had never been sure.

If two different people made a formal request, he was supposed to follow it up. Job Dawes was a big landowner as well, so maybe he shouldn't try to dodge this one. He smiled at the thought. The result of this one might be a bit different to what anyone expected. At least he might find out the real reason for his interest.

The next day John Henry sent a message to Job Dawes, simply that he would like to have another word with the farmer about the land the new baker was using on Leabrooks Road. And if it was convenient he could come back with his driver.

Job smiled at his wife. The sheriff's coach was awaiting him, and he would be visiting that dignitary. She would have to organise the staff and no, he didn't know when he would be back.

The rotund farmer looked through the door at passers-by. He even wondered if it would be seemly to wave at faces he knew, thinking they would wonder how he was on such close terms as to ride in the sheriff's coach.

The girl at the door of the mansion showed him into a side room and said, "The sheriff will see you in while, you can wait in there."

Job stood looking at the portraits of previous incumbents of the position. The last two he recognised, though the painter had certainly enhanced their good points.

He had been made to wait about half an hour before being shown into the main room, where the sheriff was seated on an elevated row of seats, a man on either side of him, neither of whom he recognised.

Job was feeling distinctly uncomfortable as he was forced to look up at them, almost as though he was a prisoner in the dock. This was nothing like the informal meeting he expected.

It was one of the other men who spoke. "Mr Job Dawes?"

"Yes."

"Now we understand you wish to make a formal complaint about someone misappropriating some of your land."

"Oh no sir, I simply enquired from John Henry about the position."

"You mean Mr Lawence?"

"Yes sir."

"You asked him just what?"

"It was a piece of common land that he had taken."

"Who had taken?"

Job was rambling something incoherent.

"You really will have to speak up Mr Dawes."

"Mr John Barlow has died sir and this man, this baker, has commandeered his land. I didn't think it was right."

"So you have nothing else to add to that?"

"No sir."

The three men sitting above him began talking amongst themselves. Job Dawes was craning his neck to get a better view of them, trying to ascertain just what they were talking about. Eventually the man who seemed to be the spokesman continued.

"You may go Mr Dawes, but I think you had better wait, at least until we reach some decision. The girl will show you to a room. If we need you again, we will fetch you."

An usher led him to the door where a young woman took over and showed him back to the room where he had previously waited.

Job Dawes found his legs were trembling and that he was wet from sweat. This was outside anything he had experienced. This had been a bigger ordeal than he had expected. He spoke to the austere-looking female.

"I felt like a criminal back there."

She didn't help with his peace of mind, just looking down her long, hooked nose, and over the spectacles lodged on the bridge. She didn't answer his remark, just saying, "You will wait there, Mr Dawes, until you are called again, or are allowed to go."

He opened his mouth to reply, thought better of it, and slumped miserably on to a hard bench and waited. He would have been surprised if he had seen all the other people waiting to enter the room in which the dignitaries were waiting to question them.

The vicar of Alfreton was next in.

"Good of you to come Mr Howard. We would just like to ask you a few questions about Mr John Barlow." The speaker was the same man who had just questioned Job Dawes.

William Howard knew the purpose of the elevated seating, it was the same principle employed by the church, but he felt less intimidated than Job Dawes had done.

"Mr Barlow died several months ago and was interred in the churchyard at my church. His home address was given as Ironville. The church fees were paid for in a sealed envelope delivered to the church prior to the funeral. There were no mourners."

"You seemed to have your answer well prepared vicar."

"I have been asked the same question before, by you, and so had checked the facts."

"Wasn't it unusual to have the burial paid for in an envelope, by unknown hand, when there were no mourners?"

"A little."

"Were there suspicious circumstances regarding the death."

"No."

"You seem certain of that."

"I know of nothing wrong about the death, sir."

"We could have the body re-examined."

"That is your privilege."

The three men now spoke together, but the vicar appeared undaunted at their deliberations.

The official now spoke again. "Well vicar, the purpose of asking you here today wasn't anything to do with his death. It was your practice of informing certain individuals about such deaths so they can claim their property."

"I wouldn't do such a thing."

Again there was a conversation between the three men.

"It seems we have had more than one complaint to that effect."

"You have not done me the courtesy, sir, of informing me so that a thorough check of my staff could be made, and I could take what disciplinary action I thought necessary."

"The complaints were made against you sir." This time it was the High Sheriff who spoke.

"Then I hotly deny them, in their entirety."

"Then you will have to see that nothing else of the kind happens that causes further complaints to be made, or we will be forced to follow up on them."

"What exactly do you mean by that?"

"I think you know exactly what I mean, and I wouldn't want anything to happen that would bring disgrace to your office."

The vicar started to speak, spluttered a little, then looking at the raised hand of the man seated above his head, thought

better of it and said nothing.

He sat stoically looking at the stony faces of the men facing him, and perhaps for the first time in his life didn't feel that he was getting the best of an argument.

The Reverend William Howard of St Martin's church in Alfreton remained quiet and waited as the three men spoke amongst themselves for several minutes, before the man on the right said, "Right Mr Howard, you can go. Perhaps you would be good enough to wait for a little while, the usher will escort you."

The vicar was also led to a vacant room by the stony-faced woman.

George Rhodes was the next to be led into the room.

"Now Mr Rhodes, we are trying to ascertain the exact ownership of a piece of former common land, in the village of Somercotes, following a complaint originally brought to our notice by yourself, but since by others. We would like to know just what your interest is in this land."

"Any complaint by me was simply a case of common justice."

"Did you know Mr John Barlow?"

"No sir."

"Do you know Mr Joseph Carlin?"

"I certainly know him by sight, and I was concerned about his activity in this case."

"In what way, sir?"

"I didn't think it was his land, and I asked if it could be investigated."

"You were sufficiently concerned to make an appointment at the office of the sheriff at your own expense, and to ask for an inquiry to be made?"

"Yes sir."

"Very public-spirited of you."

"In my experience people don't do that sort of thing, unless there is some other motive."

"That is quite so, Mr Rhodes."

The three men on the bench again had an informal talk between themselves. The man on the right then asked the farmer if there was anything he wanted to add.

"No sir, except that I drew up the plans for the development on the land, which made me suspicious of the actual ownership, that is all."

"Right, the usher will show you to the door. We have another enquiry to make, then we might need you back, if you would be kind enough to wait. You will be shown a suitable reception room."

Joseph Carlin was the next person to enter into the inquiry chamber. He had less idea than the others as to why he was there, thinking that it was in connection with the bread he had donated to the sheriff's household.

Again it was the man on the right who was the spokesman.

"Mr Joseph Carlin?"

"Yes sir."

"Do you know why we have asked you to come today?"

"Not really."

"Right, we have been asked to investigate a claim that you are conducting a business from land belonging to Mr Job Dawes."

For the first time alarm bells began ringing in his head.

"I know no one of that name sir."

"The gentleman has said he had no approach from you to purchase the land situated on Leabrooks Road at Somercotes."

"No sir, I believed the owner of the property was a Mr John Barlow from whom I obtained the land. And I have documents drawn up by a Mr Ben Smith of *Obadiah Watkins, Smith and Belton*, the respected firm of solicitors from Heanor."

"I suppose you are in possession of this very document, and that this Mr Smith, or someone at his firm, will verify its legality?"

"Yes sir, I have, and I have known Mr Smith for years. I am sure there will be no problems."

"I understand other transactions have been carried out through this legal establishment."

"That is quite correct sir."

"Just when was this purchase made Mr Carlin?"

"Some time in March, I believe."

"And how did you know Mr Barlow?"

"He approached me and offered to sell the land."

"Did he actually sign the papers himself?"

"He made his mark sir."

"And was Mr Barlow in good health at that time?"

"He seemed in poor health, and because of that he wanted to get rid of the land."

"We understood he was in good health, right up to the time of his death."

"Perhaps it was just a common cold, or something, I don't know."

"And what was your connection with Mr Barlow, why did he approach you concerning transferring his holdings?"

"I don't remember how we met, but he was aware of my interest in starting a bakery and dairy."

"And what was the nature of Mr Barlow's work, Mr Carlin?"

"I am really not sure sir."

"I see. You didn't know him well, you don't know what he did for a living, but he just approached you in this philanthropic manner because he wanted you to build a dairy and a bakery. It all seems a little unlikely."

"That is the way it was sir."

"Do you know Mr William Howard?"

"No sir."

"Others say that Mr Howard, vicar of Alfreton, passed on the very information that allowed you to steal this property, that should really belong to Mr Dawes, a farmer and holder of the adjoining former common land. And that you got a Mr George Rhodes to draw up the plans to build the said bakery and dairy."

"Not George Rhodes sir."

"Then is there someone else that you would like to implicate?"

"No sir, I have acted in good faith in all my dealings. I simply wanted to follow my ambition to make a business that would add prestige to the area."

Nevertheless, a lot of his natural composure was beginning to evaporate.

"It would appear that most of the people do not support your evidence. We will have to contact your solicitors in Heanor, it may be that they will have some awkward questions to answer."

"I am sure that Mr Ben Smith will support me sir."

"Then we will question Mr Smith."

The three men began talking amongst themselves, but Joseph couldn't catch anything they said. Again it was the spokesman on the right who addressed him.

"Do you wish to call any other witnesses to support your evidence? But before you do so, I will have to warn you that it is a serious thing to offer any evidence to this, or any other inquiry, that is untrue. It is called perjury."

"I was unaware that this was a court of law sir."

"No, it is an unofficial inquiry, but it may lead to more serious proceedings."

"I didn't know that I had committed any crime sir."

"It is just possible that you haven't, but at this stage your position is rather, shall we say, tenuous. For the moment we will have to detain you for further questioning. Take him to the inner holding cell."

He turned to the usher.

"All the other witnesses are free to go, but I shall address them all together before they are released," the High Sheriff said.

"What other witnesses?" Joseph asked, now more that a little alarmed.

But two other men behind him now held his arms and he was led away to an inner holding cell.

"What is going to happen now?" he asked his escort, but received no reply.

Joseph Carlin was far from calm now. In fact he was looking for any way he could evade his captors, but of course none presented itself. The inner holding cell was nothing more than a room, not particularly unpleasant, but secure for all that.

Behind him, and brought in from various directions, the other witnesses appeared. All seemed startled to see just who else had been questioned that day. When they were seated they had the chance to speak amongst themselves, or remain quiet if that was their wish.

The usher waited until they became fairly quiet. Then in a loud, authoritative voice said, "Quiet please!"

Instantly there was a deadly hush.

The sheriff cleared his throat with a cough and began. "Because I have been requested by more than one person, I have this day conducted an inquiry into a piece of former common land, on Leabrooks Road in Somercotes, with a view to ascertaining who in fact is the actual owner. I have asked Mr Carlin to remain here whilst we consult others, who are also implicated in this transaction. At this time, I must say that none of you gentlemen have come out of this exactly completely clean. In fact there is a vestige of self-interest in every one of you. If this had been a court of law instead of an unofficial inquiry I would have considered sending the lot of you off to the penal colony in Botany Bay."

There was a murmuring of protest among the group before him, before the usher again demanded silence.

The commanding voice continued, "Do any of you wish to say anything else at this time? If not, for now you are free to go, but I may need to call on some, or all of you, at a later date."

Job Dawes said, "I don't think this is fair. After all, I reported to you that something unseemly was happening, and it was my land that had been stolen."

"It was not your land Mr Dawes. We have taken the opportunity to examine the land registry maps. This parcel of land seemed to be sandwiched between your land and that of the squire, the late Mr Henry Case-Morewood, and there is no doubt that John Barlow had title deeds to it. So it would appear that you are one of the people trying to steal land that doesn't belong to you."

"Has anyone else anything to say? If you wish, I will list case by case, the position of each and everyone of you, either separately or in a group."

The rest of the group was now very silent and not a little crestfallen. No one realised that the authorities would make such a thorough review of the facts. All of them wanted no more than to get away from this place.

The usher now showed them to the door where they made their way outside to find their own way back to their homes. The fact that no one was to be given a comfortable ride home, and they were compelled to walk, didn't bother them in the least.

Mr Obadiah Watkins, senior partner in the noted and long-established local law firm, was called later that very day to explain the conduct of his partnership. The result was the summary resignation of Mr Ben Smith, and the disassociation of the firm from one of its partners.

Joseph Carlin was released from his enforced incarceration and shortly afterwards left the area.

Later on, Mr George Rhodes, the man who had drawn up the deeds to the property and whose position seemed at least as dubious as any of the others involved in the case, took over the premises, building the dairy and running the business until his death in the year 1857, at which time it passed to his son Mr Joseph Rhodes.

Joseph never had a liking for the trade and five years later transferred the premises back to his friend and former partner Mr Joseph Carlin.

Chapter 5

Joseph Carlin had been dubious when approached by the other Joseph, but when he found that the offer was genuine, he had warmed to the idea. Now thirty-eight, his life hadn't been anything like as financially rewarding as he would have predicted.

The scam with the vacant properties had been closed to him, and he always had the impression that the law was keeping a close eye on him. The brush with the sheriff's office had scared him more than he would have admitted. It had taken him a long while to get over that and, of course, his money had all gone on the construction work.

Then later, when he had found out that it had been George Rhodes, not his erstwhile friend, who had drawn up the plans for the bakery and dairy, he had the feeling of being undermined, as if they had together deliberately tried to thwart him.

Joseph had never married and had tried his hand at a lot of different jobs, all hard work with little reward. Then, at the beginning of 1862, he had run into the other Joseph.

Joseph Rhodes was bent double with some sort of rheumatic problems and walking painfully with the aid of a stout oak stick. He had at first not been at all sympathetic, believing he had got just what he deserved. Eventually, though, he had been persuaded that it had all been orchestrated by the older Rhodes.

Quite obviously Joseph Rhodes was in no position to run anything. Eventually, after listening first to the offer to come and run the place, then, why not be a partner, it was when the offer became, I will make it over to you at a very competitive price which you can pay when you are able to, that the offer became too good to resist. Joseph Carlin moved in.

The tenure in office of that sheriff had long been over and anyway he, Joseph, had never been charged with anything that could be described as vaguely illegal. And in a period of eighteen years there were few around who would be able to remember who had actually built the bakery and dairy at Leabrooks Road.

After a nervous start Joseph had warmed to his position as the owner of the bakery. He began to think, for the first time in years, of the attractiveness of his taking a wife to add to his status as a businessman. His choice fell on Clara-Bell Johnson, a comely girl who was a regular customer in his shop.

Little did he know that the flighty teenager had set her sights on him as soon as he arrived at the shop.

They married very soon after he had started in business, and within a month Clara-Bell announced her pregnancy. Almost straight away she abandoned any pretence of doing any work, insisting that her mother moved in to look after her.

Helen Johnson waggled in, some twenty-plus stones of wobbly jelly. Far from helping with anything she had brought another girl to wait on the pair of them, whom Helen and Clara-Bell seemed to spend all their days screaming at.

Her name was Daisy, and all day long there was a constant shout of Da--s---ee, do this, or do that. Clara-Bell soon grew as fat as her mother and she demanded to be waited on hand and foot, while filling her face with as many cream buns as she could cram in.

It wasn't long before Joseph was turned out of his bed by the constant demands of his new and very pregnant wife. Fortunately there were plenty of other rooms in the house that could be turned into bedrooms.

The business was prospering, thanks to the considerable talents of its owner, who contented himself with the thought that after the birth he would turf out this menagerie of his wife's family. He would then insist that she conducted herself as the wife of a businessman should. If she needed help with the child, this he would consider, but it certainly wouldn't be the screaming mountain of idleness that was her mother.

At barely eight months after their marriage Clara-Bell took to her birthing bed. The doctor was called who passed her on to a woman who would see to her needs. But it would be three days of total agony before a tiny baby emerged from that mountain of blaspheming blubber, who was still cursing all mankind for the indignity she had endured.

Although the child was undoubtedly slightly premature, Joseph could count as well as the next man and he resolved to have it out with his wife as soon as she was strong enough to face the pertinent questions he would ask. But long before then he intended to get rid of his mother-in-law from hell.

The midwife found a suitable wet nurse as soon as it became obvious that Clara-Bell was unable to fulfil her mothering duties, and the baby thrived.

About seven days after the birth, and long before her husband had a chance to have his little talk with her, Clara-Bell died. It was totally unexpected. Daisy had sat her up in bed, propped up with pillows, and been feeding her with her favourite cream buns. She hadn't even asked after her baby, or her husband. Her ordeal was over, now she intended to live a life of luxury and be waited on.

Daisy had gone outside to get some more buns when she heard a bump. Her mistress had overbalanced and now lay by the side of the bed. She hadn't called out and must have been dead when she reached the ground. No, Daisy hadn't tried to lift her up, she wouldn't have been able to anyway. All she could do had been to fetch help.

When the doctor arrived he had said her heart had given out. The excessive weight had been a contributing factor, and the strain of the birth had been too much.

"Why, if the birth was the cause, hadn't she die at the time?" Joseph asked.

"There is a lot we still don't know about why these things happen. Some say it's God's will," the doctor replied.

"Or the devil taking his own," Joseph muttered.

The doctor looked up sharply but didn't reply.

The body of Clara-Bell Carlin was interred at Alfreton church just two days after the death. A special, extra large coffin had to be made to contain the remains. That great mound of flesh was already beginning to smell, indeed there were those who said that the putrid stench lingered for days around the graveyard.

Apart from the insidious mutterings of Helen Johnson, there was none to question her daughter's sudden death. Clara–Bell wasn't very popular anyway, and death was too common an occurrence to warrant more than a casual comment.

Daisy was kept on as housekeeper and Joseph Carlin doted on his little daughter. She grew up pretty as a picture, with blonde curly hair, totally unlike the black hair Joseph had and the dark brown of her mother.

Joseph had her christened Sara after his own mother, but his mother-in-law wasn't even told of the ceremony. And he left instructions that if she ever arrived she wasn't to be allowed anywhere near his daughter

It was said that the bakery and dairy, with its own made butter and cheese, was the talk of the area with visitors coming from miles away just to buy and taste *Joseph's* bread or cheese. There were other bakers around but it was *Joseph's* that was the attraction.

Joseph Carlin was proprietor of the business for a further fourteen years, then in the year 1876 he sold it. Rather he passed it on to his two assistants, Harry Kane and John Sergeant. Sara had shown no interest in the business so he set her up as a dressmaker, which suited her to a tee.

Joseph retired at the age of 56 in an age when retirement was almost unheard of. He went to live in Newark in the neighbouring county of Nottinghamshire, where he was described as a gentleman.

A New Ear (Chapter 1)

When it was known that Joseph was going to retire, do nothing and be a gentleman, it was the talk of the area. People just didn't do 'nothing'! They worked, and then they died.

The bakery and the dairy were going to be split up. John Sergeant was having the bakery and Harry Kane would be running the dairy. Nominally they were partners, but each would run his own half. However, it would still be just the one firm.

The two men had worked for Joseph, so they would just be carrying on as they had done, but now they were their own bosses.

But of course the place was much more than just the bakery and dairy. It was a whole self-contained unit. There was what Joseph called the livestock. They had the goat to give them the milk for the cheese, they had chickens and they sold the eggs, and they had pigs, which they grew and slaughtered all on the same premises.

Everyone worked at everything, with the guiding hand of Joseph controlling everything. There was little wonder Harry and John, now cast adrift to stand or fall by their own initiative, were apprehensive. Joseph did all the buying-in. He sorted out all the prices. Now that guiding hand would be removed.

It wasn't as if he had given any indication of what he intended to do. They hadn't been initiated into the difference between being a worker and a master.

Yes, Harry and John were bewildered, not a little frightened, like a rabbit caught in the headlights as it were. Even so, when the shock finally died down they were excited. This was a chance that came to few in the eighteen-hundreds.

The organization that Joseph had built up was extensive. Harry Kane was responsible for the pigs and the chickens, the daily collection and the selling of the eggs, and the eventual slaughtering of the pigs. Indeed he had to know just when to do this.

Then there were goats, tethered behind the stables. These weren't even on bakery land, but no one had questioned the fact that goats happily chomp at anything that grows. The extensive nettle beds had already been disposed of, before the goats had been moved to devour the bracken and scrubs. Now they were somewhat further away in some more thistles and nettles. Joseph had always said that the milk tasted better when their diet consisted of at least some nettles.

Nominally they had moved from the edge of farmer Dawes' property onto the squire's land. No one complained, they were probably glad to see the back of such unprofitable crops.

However, it was also Harry's job to fetch and to milk the animals, and to turn this into cheese and butter. Strangely, he hadn't thought anything of it when he had been an employee. He had happily done each task in turn at the behest of his employer. Now, oddly however, he wondered just what to do next. He was almost like a fish out of water floundering at his responsibility. Gradually he settled down to it though.

The dairy, situated on the front of the building next to the road, served as a shop as well. So he had to leave off to serve any customer.

John Sergeant was the baker and he had to be up and in his bakery by four each morning mixing and kneading his doughs. He now had the extra task of ordering all his ingredients, as well as selling, organising his delivery boy, and making sure that the horse was stabled and fed.

Any wastage on the bread side was used to fatten the pigs. For the present this was all right, but it would be a bone of contention when, as did happen in the future, the place was split.

Whatever financial arrangements, if any, had been made for buying the business was not in the public domain, though it was known that an ongoing loan of £750, an enormous sum, remained on the books. And this was still there years later when Joseph finally died.

Both men missed the steadying influence of Joseph and, at first, both acted as if he would be back, but gradually they settled down.

Both were industrious and hard working and, if anything, profits continued to rise.

Then John decided to marry, his bride was Dorothy King. She was dark-haired, hook-nosed and haughty in the extreme. She was taller than either of the partners, indeed taller than most of the customers, and she had the unfortunate habit of holding her head back, which gave the impression of looking down her nose at almost everyone she spoke to.

She came to serve in the shop and soon decided that as there were two people in their family working in the firm, as against just Harry Kane, so they should have double the

financial rewards. And as the bakery was taking a bit more than the dairy, this reinforced her argument.

The horse and dray, which was out each day, delivered mainly bread, though there were a few pats of the goat butter and cheese, and a few eggs. The dray-boy drew his wage out of the joint funds. Harry wasn't happy with this, but eventually he did get the concession that the dray-boy's expenses came out of the bakery funds. He still argued that this hadn't been the agreement, or what Joseph would have wanted. But Dorothy also had a loud voice, and in conjunction with her domineering personality, this completely drowned out his reasoning.

To even out the proceedings Harry decided he had to marry. His eye settled on Faith Benedict, small, with blonde curly hair, and a pleasant personality. Like her own family, she was highly religious, but what had drawn him to her in the first place was that fact that she was quietly spoken. In fact the complete opposite to his partner's wife. He certainly didn't want a loud-mouthed woman like his partner had acquired. It was noticeable that John said less and less. That woman drowned out anything he tried to say, until he simply let her get on with it.

Harry and Faith married at Alfreton's St Martin's church, on a Sunday between the morning and the evening services. It wasn't normal, but the vicar agreed to conduct the ceremony. Her parents were friends of his and his church. It wasn't just that they attended church more often than anyone else, the late eighteen-hundreds was a particularly religious period. Disease was rampant, cholera, tuberculosis, diphtheria, the plague, and a score of obscure infections carried many to an early grave. In the main, life was short, brutal and abrupt. Everyone was in fear for their immortal soul, and because of this all the religious houses were full every

Sunday. Even if the pubs and ale-houses were just as full later on, and drunkenness and lewd songs were the norm.

Harry had made a generous donation to the church so maybe that was more the consideration in the vicar's mind. The church was bedecked with flowers the day was warm and everything added to the occasion. It was noticeable that Dorothy Sergeant didn't stay till the end. Someone said, "It looks as if someone's put her nose out of joint."

"And what a nose to put out of joint," came back the reply, amidst loud laughter.

The Kane's moved in above the dairy. They made the place comfortable and, though it was a little cramped, they were happy in their little love nest. Frankly, they didn't care that the Sergeants had the main house just behind the shop. Still Dorothy didn't want it to be an equal share.

The bakery sales began to shrink, mainly because Mrs Sergeant wasn't at all popular, and the pleasant Mrs Kane helped to increase the butter and cheese sales.

In the finish it became obvious that the only solution would be to separate the two businesses. They were separate anyway, in all but name. The financial division had been made long ago.

At this time, the dairy sales were beginning to outstrip those of the bakery. This would be to the benefit of the Kanes and Dorothy Sergeant wanted some compensation. She was loud in her condemnation of their former partners. "They are always trying to rob us," she complained, bitterly.

After one particular rant, Faith Kane simply said quietly, "You have got the main house, you have a larger share of the property. Perhaps we should let a lawyer decide what is a fair division. You must also have noticed that we have been contributing the larger share of the profits lately."

Even John smiled behind his wife's back.

She turned to him for support, but for once he was having none of it and said, "Isn't it about time you gave it a rest. Faith is right, just remember this, 'A house divided against itself cannot stand'."

"John!" she gasped, but it was more a note of resignation.

John Sergeant just walked away, and then so did Faith.

Harry, when he heard about the exchange later, said, "I bet he doesn't have a very nice home to go to tonight."

Faith became pregnant almost at once and there seemed an even greater contrast between the two couples. Faith and Harry radiated their obvious happiness, the other couple appeared to have the weight of the world on their shoulders.

Little Harry was born in October of 1877. He was a happy little chap, with an infectious burst of laughter whenever something amused him. As he grew bigger it seemed always Mrs Sergeant who was the butt of his laughter. He took to stroking his nose then throwing his head back.

"Don't let her see you doing that," his father warned him, "or she will give you a bat behind your ears."

About this time the milk from the goats seemed to dry up, so Harry just slaughtered them and sold the meat. Next he substituted them with a couple of cows and these were housed in the back, left-hand corner of the property, that is to say, behind the pigs and hens.

Now, when he took them to graze on the land behind the bakery there was an immediate howl of protest. No one had minded the goats who happily grazed on nettles and thistles, but cattle were a different thing altogether. Their chosen food was grass which was a cash crop to the landowners. Harry finally had to request grazing at the farm opposite. This was next to the horse-mill, which was a new place set up just opposite the bakery to grind the corn. Harry had to pay for grazing at the farm, usually in his dairy produce. But one way or another, the move to cows instead of the goats didn't seem such a good idea.

Everyone knew that people sometimes got ill when they had cow's milk or cow's cheese, but never if it was milk from the goats. That was one reason why Joseph insisted on the goats. It was strange that Harry had believed that no one would notice the difference. People didn't drink water or cow's milk, which was why alcohol was the drink of the people, and why alcoholism was rife, in the nineteenth century.

Young Harry grew up, was an industrious chap, and eventually began working in the dairy. A little sister was born when Harry was about six. She had begun to show signs of being just like her brother.

"Why did you wait so long?" customers asked. Or, "Was she a mistake?"

"Oh no," Faith would reply. "We wanted loads of kids, they just didn't come along, that's all."

When Mary was six and already showing signs of being something of a scholar, she contracted influenza and was very ill in bed. The doctor was called and he said, "All you can do is keep her warm, give her plenty of fluids, and nothing to eat," quoting the age-old saying, 'You feed a cold and starve a flu'. He left some evil-smelling concoction which she was to take each hour. "Within thirty-six hours we will see which way it's going."

"But Mary is only six years old."

"Yes, she is strong and healthy but, as always, she is in the Almighty's hands. Sometimes God calls the best ones the soonest."

"Then I will never trust in God's mercy again."

"Mrs Kane, I know you don't believe that, I was just preparing you for any scenario."

The tear-lined face was hard as she looked up, "I meant every word doctor."

"Then I suggest that you go and pray for your immortal soul Mrs Kane."

"I will wait doctor Jones, if you don't mind, to see if it is worth the effort."

Mary did get over whatever had afflicted her but it took a long while, and her face seemed to have developed a sort of twitch and she became more withdrawn and quiet. She was still a lovely little girl, but something was different. As she grew older she became the butt of jokes, and the more it happened the more nerves she developed.

Harry stood up for her and one day he came home with a black eye for his trouble. His mother was upset, but his father said it was all part of growing up.

Little Mary was upset though. "It isn't right that Harry should get his eye in such a mess, just standing up for me."

"It's all right Sis, I'd do a lot more than that for my lovely Sis."

Dorothy Sergeant was overheard to say, "Well they can't expect everything to always go their way, it's time they had their fair share of problems."

Faith told the twisted woman, "I wouldn't have expected anything else from a bitter, jealous, barren woman like you."

A little later on John came round and said, "That was a bit over the top. Dorothy always wanted children, it just didn't happen for her, and she is really upset by what you said."

"Look John, ever since I married Harry I have had to put up with snide remarks and efforts to undermine us. It's not your fault, I am sorry for you, but it was always me and Harry on the receiving end. And to come out with, 'it was time something happened to us' was also a bit much. All we tried to do was to make the place work for us all, and if she really thinks what's happened to little Mary is our come-uppance then I don't want to do anything else for her, ever again."

"I don't think she means it. It's just her way."

"She does mean it though, every time."

After that, Faith had even less contact with the Sergeants. John did his best to patch up the rift but Faith, though civil with John, pointedly ignored his wife. The atmosphere became distinctly more and more strained.

To make things worse, new laws now made all children have a basic education. Because of this Mary now had to go to the local school. Once there, poor little Mary was getting bullied more frequently, and her face began twitching more and more.

The Kanes began keeping her away from school, then the school bobby called on them and, though sympathetic, insisted that Mary must have an education. Eventually, because she was getting further behind with her lessons, a private tutor was engaged. Her name was Sarah. She wasn't really a teacher, as such, but she had a boy of her own of about the same age as Mary, and she picked up what he was taught at school, passing it on to Mary.

It seemed an odd situation. There she was taking her own boy to school to be taught by others, and then coming to try to teach Mary. But it seemed to work reasonably well.

Meanwhile, in a business sense, the whole situation continually deteriorated. The partners seemed to be forever wrapped up in their own problems and the business suffered as a result.

John Sergeant said to Harry one day, "I know how things are Harry, and I sympathise, I really do, but some time we will just have to sit down and have a long talk about the business. Sales are badly down and we will have to decide how we are going to carry on."

"Do what you think John, I trust you to do whatever's right."

It seemed as if people were keeping out of the way, with no one knowing just what to say. Sales were still going down.

Around this time, Alfreton town council, with the connivance of the major landowners throughout the area, had in its wisdom decided that the surrounding villages and hamlets should be joined to the local government district of Alfreton. It was to be an alliance of equals. Neither the town nor the villages would be the dominant partner, and it was carefully worded to that effect.

Several of the villages, like Somercotes and Riddings, were larger than the town, and the main industry was also situated in the outlying areas. But the way it was put to the locals was that a larger authority would be in a better position to borrow money to put in new drainage and a clean running water supply. Now the prospect of clean running water, and the elimination of the foul drainage system, overrode any other consideration.

No progress had been made throughout the area during the previous thirty years and rampant disease emanated from the inadequate sewage systems. Many of the brooks were still the only way of carrying away the local effluences.

Rats, which were everywhere, were regarded as no more than a nuisance and no connection with health problems, which plagued the area, were even realized.

Little or no effort had been made to repair the roads since the great toll road building program of forty or fifty years before, and great water-filled ruts were everywhere.

The larger authority would be able to borrow money to install this proper water supply, which was the first step to an efficient drainage system. Only then could, and would, the roads be sorted out.

This was the argument, and with very little opposition, it was all agreed. No one seemed to have considered how, or who, would be responsible for the repayment of the large sums that would be needed.

There were soon trenches all over the place, either for the drainage or the incoming water supply, although most people didn't follow what was happening. But the whole project was completed with a minimum of delay, so the workers, or their bosses, obviously understood what was happening.

Before the already installed water could run into either houses or businesses, people had to have taps fitted, and everyone would have to pay for the taps. The authorities had conveniently failed to mention this point. Now there were howls of protest. It seemed that everyone believed, in fact they had been told, the whole thing was going to be totally free.

John Sergeant was among the first to say he had a perfectly good well, the water was clear, he was used to the system of ladling water from the depths, and he wouldn't be buying the taps.

The council sent their own inspectors to each residence, or business, and with little ado declared every well to be contaminated. Every single one would have to be either capped or filled in. John had his capped, this being the cheapest option.

The council had got its way and running water from then on became the norm. The health of the locals did improve, if not the temper, but this was a gradual thing. No one connected it with the new, more sanitary conditions. One and all believed they had been robbed and the council had made every household foot the bill for the water supply.

It was just after this time when the doctor called and asked after Mary. Firstly he tried to reassure Faith. "You know she is a wonderfully healthy girl, really quite pretty. Perhaps it might be better if she started to go back to school, where she would learn to interact with other children."

Mary was definitely withdrawn and shied away from other children. And she had the tendency to hold her head down so that no one saw her face. In truth, the twitch in her face was only evident when she came in contact with someone she hadn't seen for a while, or another child, or if she happened to see Mrs Sergeant. When alone, or with her own family, it went totally unnoticed.

Then Doctor Jones turned to face Faith. "The vicar couldn't help noticing that neither you nor your family have been at church for a while. He wondered if you were all right."

"I am perfectly all right, doctor, in fact we are all perfectly well. You may thank the Reverend Tucker for his concern." Her tone was frosty.

The doctor tried again. "You seem so wrapped up in yourself, why don't you try to go out a little? You would enjoy it at church, everyone asks after you, you have so many friends."

"I am quite all right as I am. Mary's all right as well, we don't want to go out."

"Have you considered trying for another baby?"

"Doctor, I'm sure you are a busy man, and I have plenty to do, so if you will excuse me." With that, Faith started to cut up pats of cheese. It was a speciality they had started and it had proved very popular.

The doctor looked towards her back, before turning to go.

Harry came in at that moment. "I think the doctor is going, Faith."

"Goodbye doctor," she replied, without turning round.

The door closed.

Faith turned to face her husband. "I suppose you asked him to come," she accused.

"Not entirely, he came for his cheese, and was asking about how you were."

"All you needed to say was, I am all right."

"But you are not, none of us are."

"And there is nothing he, or anyone else, can do about it."

"I'm sorry, I just don't know what to do."

"Did you tell him I should have another baby, so we could ditch Mary, and start again?"

"No, I didn't, I wouldn't."

Harry went to put his arms around his wife but she turned her back to him.

"Oh Faith, what is happening to us?"

But she just stood there with her back to him.

"I love you Faith, and I love the kids, what is happening to us?"

By now it was young Harry who was virtually running the firm. Neither of his parents seemed to have their minds on anything.

On the bakery side it was Mrs Sergeant who people wanted to avoid. But with the terrible atmosphere everywhere people were just staying away.

It was around this time that Joseph Carlin died and was to be buried at the local cemetery. The partners closed the place for the afternoon out of respect. The two men attended the burial, which turned into one of the biggest funerals in the area for a long time, reflecting Joseph's popularity, but their wives stayed away. Neither could bear to walk with the other. This caused still more gossip.

When the two men were alone together John said, "I had been thinking of going to see Joseph for a while now, it was just that it was so far away, so I never made it."

"Why, did you want to complain about me and Faith not pulling our weight?"

"No", he said, resignedly. "I wondered how he was, but he always seemed to be able to sort out these bits of problems."

"We used to be able to talk things through, what's happened to us now?"

"It's not us, it seems as if wives rule the roost now. We shouldn't have married."

"I love Faith, and I would do anything for her."

"I know Harry, maybe it's no one's fault, it's just circumstances."

"In which case not even Joseph could have done anything."

"Look, before we go, let's have a drink together, and just a little talk."

"What about?"

"I'd like to think that it didn't matter what friends talked about."

The pair didn't stay long, didn't really say anything about the business, but both, if asked, would have said it had been worthwhile.

Joseph had made a will, but had named as executors the two local publicans from the *Horse and Jockey* and the *Three Horseshoes*, perhaps reflecting his preferences. Unfortunately, as often happens with long-living individuals, he had out-lived both named individuals by a good few years. Joseph hadn't bothered to alter anything and so the will would remain in abeyance for a good many years. Whether this had any bearing on the property, no one seemed to know.

For a while, it was if the partners were waiting for the proverbial knock on the door, someone come to complain, or at least explain, just what would be going to happen next. It didn't come.

Young Harry wanted to put up a sign to tell people about the bakery and dairy. There were now quite a few other bakeries in the area, but *Joseph's* (it still went under that name) was the most impressive.

Again it was Dorothy who didn't want it. "We can't afford to spend money on putting up silly signs," she said.

Young Harry insisted, "It will pay for itself, and we will have the benefit for years to come."

"We don't want it," Dorothy insisted.

"I suppose we could have a sign saying 'The Dairy'," young Harry said to his dad.

"We could, but then she would say we are taking all the trade."

Dairy sales were keeping reasonably high. Even though the milk and cheese were down they still had the eggs, and Harry's meat was as tender as any in the area. It was also mainly because Harry was pleasant, and there wasn't another dairy locally. Even so, the atmosphere wasn't too good about the place, and bakery sales had taken a real nosedive. The worse the sales became, the more of an atmosphere settled around the whole place.

Eventually they stopped the delivery dray, it just didn't pay the lad's wage.

John said to Harry one day, "If things don't pick up we will soon have to close the bakery."

When he relayed the news to Faith she simply said, "I'm not surprised, that woman would turn milk sour."

But, though Faith herself was offhand, Mary seemed perfectly all right with her tutor, and with the family. She worked diligently behind the scenes, but always shunned any contact with the public. The twitch in her face just wasn't evident any more until she was surprised by someone unusual appearing.

One day the tutor suggested she brought her own little boy along. Faith's reaction was one of, "No, you know it will upset Mary."

"I don't think it would," Sarah said, "and sooner or later she will have to meet people. I think it will be to her benefit." "No," Faith said.

It was one day, some time after this exchange, when Sarah's young son Sam did come around. He had been off school with a chill. Whether this was by accident or design on his, or Sarah's part, Faith did not know. He had simply come down to see his mother.

It was while he was patiently waiting outside that the two children eventually saw each other.

"Hello," Sam said. "What's your name?"

"Mary," she had answered, almost before she had time to realize.

"I'm Sam. I was waiting for my mum, but I have to hide out of the way in case I am seen."

"Why?" she asked him.

"It's because the little girl she teaches doesn't like to see people."

By now Mary realized who he was. "Come in," she said. "I'll get her if you like or, if you'd sooner, I can show you how we make the cheese."

So it was, some ten minutes later, when Sarah came she found the two of them chatting together. When Sarah saw them, she quickly looked to see if Faith was around, then she said to her son, "You will get me sacked, if Mary's mum finds out have been here."

"It's all right Sarah, I saw him waiting and asked him to come in," Mary said.

"We had better go, I'll see you tomorrow."

"Will you come again, Sam?"

"We had better see if your mother says it's all right, she's already told me not to bring Sam." But Sarah gave her a wink.

Mary had asked her mother if Sarah could bring Sam, when the tutor arrived the next day, but Faith was dubious.

"What were you thinking of bringing your son here?" she asked Sarah, as soon as they were alone. "It's taken months to get her even to be as confident as she is now."

"I didn't bring him, he was just waiting for me, on the street. Mary saw him and went and asked him to come in."

"He shouldn't have been anywhere near."

"I'm sorry, but it went all right."

"But if might not have."

"I'm sorry Faith, but there is a whole world out there, and you can't hide her from it for ever."

"Please don't bring him again."

"Will you tell Mary, or shall I?"

When Mary heard her mother had forbidden Sam she went and sat alone in her little den.

"Now see what trouble you have caused," Faith said to Sarah.

It was only because she really needed the job that Sarah kept quiet.

Later, when both her parents were together Mary said to her father, "Are you ashamed of me as well, daddy?"

"Of course I'm not ashamed of you, what made you say that?"

"Mother said I've not got to let anyone see me, she is ashamed of me?"

"I never said anything of the sort, that was a wicked thing to say," Faith said.

"You said I can't talk to Sam and he has to keep away."

Harry was puzzled. "What is this about, and who is Sam?"

"Sam is Sarah's little boy, and mother say's I cant talk to him."

"Why not?"

"Mother's ashamed of me, she doesn't want anyone to see me."

"Oh no she isn't, your mum is proud of you."

Faith just stood there, her mouth open, as if she couldn't understand what was happening. Now she put her arm around her daughter.

"Oh Mary, how could you say such a thing, of course you can see Sam if you want to, I just thought… "

She was looking at Harry over her daughter's head.

Harry said, "Mum was trying to protect you."

Afterwards Sam started to come around when he came out of school, and the improvement in Mary was visible. She even spoke to some customers when they came for cheese, and the twitch in her face seemed almost to have gone.

It seemed odd, but as Mary came out of herself, Faith became more withdrawn. She no longer served in the shop, but generally busied herself as far as possible behind the scenes.

There were lots of mills to grind flour within the parish of Alfreton at this time, of all types, wind, water, steam. There was even a treadmill arrangement in which some hapless individual, or series of individuals, walked or ran in an effort to grind the grain. And there were some that were horse-powered. That is to say a horse had been trained to walk continuously round in circles with a pole fixed to a capstan, which turned a series of gears to operate the works and grind the corn. Such an unlikely contraption operated directly opposite the bakery and dairy. It had been established in 1871 by Ben Butler. Now the horse, either from sheer old age or because it had been driven mad by the tedium of its daily grind, suddenly dropped dead. As was the custom at that time, there was a collection arranged to try to purchase another animal to take its place.

Most people gave what they could. After all no one knew when misfortune might visit their door. Many a business had only survived by the generosity of their neighbours, and some hadn't because the owner hadn't been well enough liked.

Harry didn't use flour but, although he therefore didn't trade with that miller and didn't even have a lot of contact with him, gave what he could. But the collector happened to call upon the bakery when Dorothy Sergeant was around.

"No, we haven't got money to give away."

When this reaction became known, more people stayed away from the bakery. Later, when Ben Butler called personally to thank Harry, John had been around.

"What was that about?" he asked

"Oh, it was because, when the horse died, most people gave a little to help to buy another animal."

"Nobody asked me, or I would have given."

"Apparently they asked Dorothy and she sent them away with a flea in their ear."

"Oh the fool, what was she thinking of? I had better go and apologise to Mr Butler."

"It might be better if you sent Dorothy around instead."

Later, John went with his wife in tow and personally apologised to Ben Butler who took it graciously enough, but the damage was done. John pointedly began buying some of his flour from the horse-mill. He even became a friend of Ben's, occasionally going for a drink to the *Horse and Jockey* pub, which was now next door to the bakery.

Whether the incident with the horse was the reason or not, sales continued to be in the doldrums. The two partners tried to find out what difference, if any, Joseph's will would make to them. He had no relatives, at least he had always denied any knowledge of any, but if someone with any wealth passed away relatives always seemed to crawl out of the woodwork. Still, it was also possible that in his lengthy period of 'being a gentleman' he had spent what money he had. He could have had a mortgage on his house in Newark in which case maybe those people would claim the house and there would be nothing left.

"I suppose in that case it would be described as a negative will, nothing owing, but nothing left," Harry suggested.

"It would be a very clever thing to arrange, and it would pre-suppose you knew exactly when you would die."

"Or that there is money owed to him and the people involved are keeping quiet."

"Like us you mean."

"It would certainly be better if we knew if there were any problems or, indeed, if we were to get anything. He must have left something, even if it were only the house in Newark," John said.

"Maybe he would think we had made a mess of the bakery and dairy and he wasn't going to throw any more of his money after it," Harry replied.

"That was just one reason why I should have gone to see him."

"I know what you mean John, but it's too late now."

The contents of the will remained undisclosed months after Joseph's death, it seemed no one had pursued the matter.

Both John and Harry worked as hard as they could, sales seemed to have stabilised, but no one was making any fortunes. Then one day there was an almighty row between John and Dorothy. It was financially based, Dorothy wanted some money to spend and John told her there was nothing in the kitty. Afterwards, Dorothy seemed to have gone and tales were rife. Someone even suggested he had probably murdered her.

"I'd have dumped her in the well when it was capped," another had said. Everyone agreed that no one would have blamed him.

Faith asked Harry what he thought.

"It's nothing to do with me," Harry replied.

Faith seemed more concerned than anyone else.

"I'm frightened Harry," she said, on another occasion. More and more she asked Harry for reassurances of his love for her.

On the other hand, Mary seemed to have forgotten all her fears about her looks. The twitch appeared to have completely gone, she even went helping in the bakery shop sometimes. It was noticeable that people seemed to favour the young, pretty Mary, who was unfailingly polite and helpful. Sales started to increase for the first time in years. John wanted her to be there on a regular basis but Harry pointed out she was only eight years old, and she must legally still be in full-time education.

"It's all silly," John said. "Girls of that age used to be working down the pits, my own mother was."

"You don't want those times to come back, do you?"

"Of course not. My mother fought to keep me away from the pits, so I'd be the last one to want anyone, let alone girls, down there."

"I know that, but some as young as Mary are still down there."

"This is different, it's a nice job for a little girl in the shop, and it will help in her education."

"I'm sorry John, we had enough trouble getting her away from school, even when we provided her with a private tutor."

"Isn't she becoming a lovely girl though? If only we'd had some children, things might have been different."

Faith didn't really want her to help in to bakery shop, but Harry insisted it was all part of her getting rid of her phobia for good.

Faith was becoming more and more reclusive, staying in the house and refusing to see anyone, until Harry eventually, when the doctor called for his cheese, asked him for his advice.

"I don't know what is the matter with Faith, she doesn't want to do anything, only sit in the house."

"Does she do the housework?" he asked.

"She does some, but Mary helps as well."

Harry immediately took him to see for himself. She was sitting in the back room with the screens drawn to keep out the light. She held a pillow across her knees and her head was leaning forward, as though not wanting to see whoever entered the room. At first, none of them saw each other. Then, as the two men entered, all three looked up. The doctor went straight across towards the window and drew back the screens, exposing her to the light of day. Then he went into a rant.

"I suppose you realise this is God's work, you wilful girl. I tried to warn you, but you wouldn't listen. Look at yourself, a total wreck. Go to church, get on your knees and pray to the Almighty for His forgiveness."

He promptly left, with Harry feeling he had done more harm than good, and becoming more that a little apprehensive about Faith's reaction. There was none, leaving him more concerned than ever. This was the worse he had seen her, seeming oblivious to anything around her.

Faith became more and more like a zombie.

"Oh darling, what are you doing to yourself?"

"Can't you just leave me alone."

Harry stood there, tears streaming down his face.

Mary now came into the room and her deep blue eyes looked from one to the other. It was as if she was the only one grown-up at that minute.

"Go and do some work daddy, mummy and me will be all right."

With that she put her arm around her mother. "Come on mummy, we had better sort the cheese out, you know the men can't manage without us."

Harry was astonished when his wife stood up and was led into the larder. He walked out into the shop and as he went he rubbed a cloth across his face to clean up his distress.

A little later on Mary came into the shop.

"Is she all right?" he asked.

"Yes, she is packing up the portions of cheese. I'm sorry daddy, it was my fault, I left her a bit too long."

Harry left his son serving in the shop, put an arm around his daughter's shoulder and led her, or was led, into the back room.

"No, it was mine, I didn't realise she was quite as bad as that."

"She isn't really, it's just that she can't be left too long."

"She's all right during the night, but she is always asleep as soon as we go to bed, and when I get up."

"No, she isn't, she pretends a lot. I go and get her up as soon as you get up, and I try to be with her for as long as I can."

"But your lessons, and when you go to help in the baker's shop?"

"I set her tasks to keep her occupied, and I keep slipping back to make sure she is all right."

"How long has this been going on?"

"Oh, she hasn't been quite so bad, but since I didn't go to school, I've been looking out for her."

"But   your   eye."
"Oh, I can do that anytime."

The tears started running freely, but noiselessly, down his face again. "I've failed you both, haven't I?"

"No daddy, you are just a man and you don't understand these things."

"And your tutor, do you really need a tutor?"

"Not really, she brought me the work Sam did at school. Sarah couldn't read or write, so then I taught her."

"But Sarah was supposed to be teaching you."

"We learned it together."

"I was paying her to teach you."

"You were paying so that I didn't have to go to school, and you were getting the best of both worlds. I was looking after mummy so you didn't have any worries and I was learning at the same time. And I think you will find I am just as clever as Sam or anyone else of my age. I haven't heard John complaining when I served in his shop, so I can do figures as well as anyone. I really wanted to help John because then I knew I could do it."

"What is the use in having Sarah here at all?"

"If she wasn't, the school bobby would have carted me off to school."

"You would at least have had a proper teacher."

"Who would have looked after mummy then?"

"I would have sorted it somehow."

"No daddy, this way we have all got the best possible solution."

"Solution, where did you learn that word?"

"Someone used it in the shop, so I asked what it means."

"I am beginning to wonder just who is eight, and who is thirty-six."

The little girl fixed her big blue eyes on her father. "I am just doing what has to be done, so please leave things as they are."

"I can see young Harry doesn't need me to run the place, and you have organised everything else. What is my job now?"

"Oh, you are just daddy."

Harry looked in sheer disbelief at this child/woman.

"I think it's probably best now you know though, that's one less thing for me to bother about. And now you know, you might be able to help as well."

Harry walked back to the shop, rubbing his hand across the back of his neck. There was only young Harry in the shop when he returned. He stood watching him for a while.

"What did we ever do to make two such remarkable kids as you two?"

Young Harry looked at his father. "What is this all about?"

"Oh nothing, I was just thinking aloud."

Later, much later, when he was talking to John, he told him a little of what had happened.

"Oh, I knew there wasn't much wrong with that twitch, I sort of observed her close up. What I mean is, I knew it had gone long ago, and I knew she could do it if she wanted. I remember when that school teacher came in one day, she did it perfectly."

"You didn't think to tell me then, did you?"

"I thought you must know, and it was none of my business."

"So everyone knew I had a genius for a daughter and no one thought to tell me. I think I need a stiff drink."

Chapter 2

Helen Benedict was tending her garden. She had potatoes, beans, onions, Brussels sprouts, and all manner of spices for flavourings, and she had herbs for tending all the basic ailments. She also had soft fruit, and apples, gooseberries, blackcurrants, and any other thing she believed to be useful.

Helen believed she was entirely self-sufficient, and to spare. What she couldn't grow she could barter, even for things like meat. Her family's table was always full.

Her husband Ben had always been a carpenter and had always worked for Ben Butler (*Anything from wood*). And when Ben Butler had suggested that they upped sticks and moved out of Alfreton and into the neighbouring village of South Wingfield, he had, after a talk with his wife, quickly agreed.

It had made sense, almost all their business was in Wingfield anyway. And Ben had the chance to buy a wood yard when Israel Bartholomew had unexpectedly died and the wood yard suddenly become vacant. It was an extensive area, far better than the cramped place they had in Alfreton. The Benedicts had found this wonderful cottage and Helen had what she always wanted, a piece of land, enough room to grow whatever she wanted. It seemed to everyone that all their birthdays had come at once.

They had only the one daughter, Faith, and she was happily married now.

They hadn't wanted to be the type of parents that were forever in Faith's house. Helen remembered how she cringed when her own mother-in-law was always popping in. They were about three miles from Alfreton, and a further two from Somercotes. Oh, it was easily walkable, but the ground was a bit hilly, and without any real reason for the journey, why should they bother? If they were wanted, well Faith knew just where to find them. In the meantime better let things stay as they were.

It was a Saturday and Ben didn't usually work late at weekends, so she was expecting him home from work soon. Also, for once, he had said he wasn't likely to be late tonight, so she would go and clean up and put the finishing touches to the dinner, so that it would be ready.

A horse and buggy pulled up directly by her gate. She watched whilst someone was obviously directing the driver, then the man pointed straight up her drive. Who could possibly want to see her, or her Ben?

Intrigued now, she watched who would get out of the carriage.

The man looked familiar, but he had a coat covering him although it certainly wasn't cold today. Probably it was someone old who felt the cold more. He was walking up the path. The buggy had pulled on to a piece of ground, settling for a bit of a wait. Then she recognised him. A little older, but it was definitely the Reverend Tucker, vicar of Alfreton, and they hadn't seen him since they had left the town, more that ten years ago. Why had he come? What could be wrong? Helen hurried down the path towards him, full of a terrible apprehension.

"Vicar, what's happened?"

"Hello Helen, are you going to invite me in, it's been a bumpy ride, and I'm not so supple as I once was. And I think I swallowed all the dust there was on that track."

"Of course, but why are you here?"

"I wanted to see an old parishioner, and friend." Together they walked into the cottage. "You have a nice place here Helen, I hope you are attending church as regularly as ever."

She smiled. "Of course, but South Wingfield is nearer than Alfreton you know, and it's a nice little church. But that isn't the reason you have come after all these years, is it?"

Only when his adequate frame was comfortably settled and a cup of tea was in his hand did the vicar give any indication of why he had made his journey.

"Faith isn't."

"Faith isn't what?"

"I think Faith isn't living up to her name, she hasn't attended Sunday service for more than a year."

"You mean she is attending one of these newfangled chapels?"

"If she was, that would be bad enough, but I don't think she is even doing that. She denounced her faith because she thought that girl of hers was being called back to God's keeping. That was a few years ago, and we haven't seen her since."

"But Mary is all right now, isn't she?"

"I don't know, we haven't seen her at all."

"What does Faith say?"

"I can hardly ask unless I can't see her, can I?"

Helen eyed him quizzically.

"You wouldn't have made this journey, which you clearly didn't relish, unless there is something else you haven't told me."

"It is clearly my duty to do all I can to bring a sinner back to the fold."

"What has actually happened?"

The Reverend Tucker drank a sip of his tea, obviously in no mood to rush.

"Would you like some dinner vicar, there is plenty to share between the three of us?"

When Ben came back from work a few minutes later, he looked first at the carriage, pulled on to the uncultivated land just beyond the cottage, then hurried up the pathway to the house. He wondered if it was them who had a visitor, or someone from the row of cottages a little further up the road. Someone who could afford a carriage, and was calling at their place, probably didn't bring good tidings.

As he saw through the window the churchman's ample frame comfortably sitting on his own favourite chair, he quickened his step and pushed open the door, just as Helen placed the plate of dinner in front of him. She looked up. "Oh hello dear, the vicar's just called in for a chat."

His face mirrored his concern. Vicars didn't hire a carriage and go outside their own parishes to call in for a chat, especially after an absence of eight or ten years. Neither person attempted to elaborate, so he took off his coat and waited for whatever the explanation could be. He sat down, and Helen put his dinner in front of him, getting her own before anyone said a thing.

The Reverend Tucker, obviously a lover of good food, continued eating until his hunger was satisfied, washing the meal down with a nice glass of claret. Ben, for his part, simply picked at his meal. Only when the vicar had finished did anyone speak.

"That was enjoyable Helen," he began, "but about the other matter, I expect you to resolve that, just as satisfactorily and quickly." Totally ignoring the fact that Ben hadn't finished his dinner, he continued, "And now Ben, you can get my carriage to the gate and I will take my leave of you. I am after all a very busy man."

"Of course, vicar." Ben got up hurriedly and went outside to hail the carriage.

It was only when the vicar had finally left that Helen was able to explain the reason for his unexpected visit.

"Well, has someone died, or have we upset the vicar in some way, or aren't you going to tell me, Helen?" Ben began, as he re-entered the room, raising his eyebrows in the expectant way he did when inviting others to explain themselves.

"No dear, neither of those things. It seems the vicar is concerned about Faith's immortal soul."

Now Ben, deeply religious as he was, really was concerned.

"Come on Helen, just what could Faith possibly have done to make him leave the comforts of the vestry? I watched him get into that carriage and I know he wasn't relishing the return journey."

"It seems Faith hasn't been attending church as often as she should."

"Surely he has had it out with her?"

"No, he decided it was our duty to make sure she attended."

"That's a back-handed way of doing things, I would have thought."

"Either way he expects us to sort it out."

"Is it just her, or has all her family been wayward? I would have thought Harry would have made all his family attend in their best bib and tucker."

"He didn't make it clear, just that we had to make sure she was there."

"I suppose it was too much to expect that he would have offered us a ride in his carriage."

"He wouldn't want to make it that easy, this is to be our penance as well."

"I suppose we will have to make the walk, at least the weather isn't too bad for a walk."

Helen looked at her husband. "With my rheumatic knee I don't know if I could make it that far."

"As I see it, the vicar hasn't given us a choice."

"I suppose he will condemn Faith, and us as well, just as loudly as he can at Sunday's service if we aren't all there."

"His view will be that he has given us one last opportunity to save all our souls."

"I wonder if she has been ill? There must be some simple explanation, and he could have found that out for himself."

"You know the Reverend Tucker, he will use what he thinks is the best way to get results."

"Anyway Ben, your dinner is getting cold."

Ben Benedict, normally one to relish his food, now sat down and picked at the rest of his meal before pushing away the still half-filled plate.

"I have made a decision," he announced. "We have to go, but we haven't got to kill ourselves to get there. Like the vicar we will go by carriage."

"Where will we get a carriage from?"

"I will ask Mr Butler if I could borrow the wood cart. I'll clean it up and we will go in style."

So it was, a little later on that night, and after a whole lot of work brushing and scrubbing the wood cart clean enough so that their Sunday best wouldn't be too spoiled, that the whole Benedict family perched high on their own particular charabanc, arrived along Leabrooks Road and pulled up outside the bakery shop.

Young Harry was first to spot his grandparents as they made their somewhat ungainly way down from the height of Ben Butler's (*Anything from wood*) conveyance. With a shouted warning to his father, he went outside to offer some assistance to help them down from the cart.

"Young Harry, you are quite the man now," his granddad said. "And how is your mother?"

"She is all right," he replied.

Old Harry had followed him outside and now stood behind him.

"Are you sure of that?" the old man continued.

"Yes, why?" young Harry asked

"Come inside," his father said, "and tell us what has prompted this visit."

Now the whole lot of them traipsed straight through the shop and into the back room. Mary had heard the commotion and now joined them.

Her grandmother now spoke, "This can't be little Mary, she has grown up to be quite a young woman."

"It isn't a birthday, or some anniversary that we have forgotten, and I know you well enough to realize that there must be some purpose for your visit," Harry said.

"Can't we just come to see our only daughter?"

"Of course you can, and right welcome you are to."

"But, up to now, the only person we haven't seen is Faith. She isn't ill, is she?"

It was Mary who was the first to reply. "Mummy has gone for a lie down, she was tired."

Ben Benedict raised his eyebrows in that expressive way he had. "Never in the whole of my life have I felt the need to lie down before night time, and neither has her mother."

"Mummy gets so very tired," Mary said.

Ben looked at his son-in-law. "Just what is the matter with her Harry, what has the doctor said?"

"Faith didn't want to see a doctor, she's all right, it's just like Mary said, she gets so very tired."

"And on Sundays, is she tired every Sunday as well?"

"Why have you really come Dad?"

"It is a bit embarrassing when the vicar has to come all the way to Wingfield to tell us that our only daughter has renounced her faith."

"She would never do that."

"Then why hasn't she been to church for years, and why haven't her family either?" There was an embarrassed silence before Ben continued, "I think you had better go and fetch your mother Mary, we have to get to the bottom of this."

Mary looked at her father, hoping for some instruction but Harry didn't say anything.

"Either Faith comes to us, or we will have to go up to her."

Mary left in the direction of her mother's bedroom. Someone came into the shop so young Harry went to serve them, leaving his father alone with the grandparents.

"Are you going to offer some sort of explanation Harry, because up to now all we have heard is evasions?"

"I wish I could, she just isn't herself."

"What have you done to her?"

"I haven't done anything, I love Faith, I wouldn't do anything to stop her going to church."

"It was your duty to make her go, even if you had to carry her, and it was your duty to go yourself, and take the rest of your family."

"I know that, in an ideal world."

"Her mother and me have been worried sick since we knew."

Mary now re-entered the room. "Mummy can't get up, she feels too ill."

"She will get up, and give an account of herself." Ben Benedict pushed past his granddaughter and went towards the stairs. Mary tried to stop him but to no avail, so she followed him up the stairs.

"Please Granddad, it'll only make things worse."

Harry and his mother-in-law followed. When the procession entered her bedroom Faith tried to pull the covers over her face. But her father would have none of it and grasping the blanket, before Harry could intervene, pulled it from her and on to the floor.

Faith had tucked herself into a ball and pulled one arm over her head, but Ben Benedict was not to be denied, he had already grabbed her arm before Harry stopped him.

"What you need my girl is a good hiding, and if your husband wont discipline you, then I will."

"Please," Harry said.

He had pulled Ben backwards and caused the older man to stumble, almost losing his footing.

"Calm down Dad, let's have a talk about this."

"I think it's getting a little too late for talk my lad when the Reverend Tucker comes to my home and threatens the lot of us with eternal damnation."

"Please, sit down. No one wants this, but Faith can't bear to go out. I can't blame her if she is ill, the vicar should have come to see for himself."

"If she is ill why haven't you got the doctor?"

Mary, who had now got past the older people and was sat on the bed at her mother's side, had put her arms around her and was cradling her and was talking to her as if she were the child.

"It's all right Mummy, I wont let anyone hurt you."

Ben's anger seemed to have subsided somewhat as he surveyed the scene.

It was Helen who spoke, "Why didn't you send, if Faith needed us, and why have you let things get so bad?"

"Daddy didn't know," Mary's high-pitched voice sounded above the commotion.

"He must have known child," her grandmother said. "And he is guilty of bringing you up in this Godless house."

"I will take the children to church on Sunday," Harry said, "but Faith cannot go, not until she is better. Sarah will come in, and sit with Faith and that is my final word on the matter."

"The Reverend Tucker expects Faith to be there as well."

"I do not think a merciful God could condemn Faith for being ill, and I will invite the vicar to see for himself."

"The vicar isn't into mercy, he is more for getting results, and he isn't going to be satisfied with anything less than the whole family lined up and facing his wrath this Sunday. I fear he intends to condemn the whole lot of us from the pulpit."

"I will go to see him in the morning, before Sunday service, and plead for his and God's mercy."

"That might have sufficed before he made the journey to Wingfield, I doubt its effectiveness now."

"I can only try."

"And at Sunday service we will all be given this very public condemnation."

"You need not be there, you don't even live in the parish."

"Oh, but he is insisting that we all attend. I'm afraid he will be preparing the service even as we speak."

Faith let out a cooing sound as Mary continued to cradle her head.

"We must get the doctor, we have to try to get her better," Ben continued.

"No," it was Mary speaking, "they would lock mummy away with a lot of funny people."

"How do you know about funny people, child?" her grandmother asked.

"Sarah told me. She knew someone who went there, they never let her out again."

"Is that it Harry, are you afraid that will happen?"

"I don't know what will happen, I only want the best for my wife. I promised I would love and cherish her as long as I live, and I will do that."

"But Harry," Helen continued, "it is her immortal soul we have to protect. For her own sake she has to attend church."

"And so do you," Ben added.

Young Harry had now returned from the shop.

"And how often do you attend church?" his grandmother asked, turning to him.

Harry didn't answer, so she turned on his father.

"Don't you think this is punishment for your Godless ways?"

He replied, "We all say our prayers. Faith is a wonderful lady and she can't help being ill. Because of our work, preparing the doughs on Sunday, it is difficult to attend church. We have always given generously to the church and I can't honestly believe that God would punish us for our industry."

"It is written," his mother-in-law continued, "that God created heaven and earth in six days, even He rested on the seventh. Is your work more difficult than His?"

Harry had forgotten how religiously dogmatic Faith's parents could be, and the last thing he wanted was an argument. He remained silent.

Believing she had won the exchange, and waxing to her theme, she continued, "To suggest that it is more important to make bread on the Sabbath than to do God's work shows just how depraved you have become. I'm not surprised that the Reverend Tucker has despaired of you."

"As I said, I will go and see the vicar. I will do my best to make him realise why we haven't been at Sunday service and after that it is up to him, and the God he serves."

"That is blasphemous."

"No Mother, that is common sense, and I can only hope that God sees it the same way."

"I can see now why you haven't been insisting all your family attend church each Sunday. Father and I haven't missed a service in forty years."

"We all serve in whatever way we can. I have contributed in any way possible, financially or with my time, to provide things for the church."

"Don't you see, the Lord wants you not your money."

"When the vicar wants a new church roof he is happy enough to accept my donations."

"Can't you even see why Faith is sick?"

"People get sick Mother, and some even die, with or without attending God's house."

"But afterwards, it is the righteous who enter God's kingdom."

"Mother, oh Mother, you should see some of the terrible people who go to church, and some of those who do not. I cannot believe that any god would discriminate just because some go to church and some do not."

"It is written… "

"I am sure it is, but men wrote the book, not some divinity."

"The devil has possessed you Harry Kane."

There was a stand off. Neither was going to win this argument.

"As I said Mother, I will go and see the vicar. I will explain why we haven't been at Sunday service, what happens then is up to him."

"The Reverend Tucker insists you will all be there, and us as well."

"We will see, I can do no more."

"The Reverend Tucker came all the way to Wingfield to insist that you are there, and he will accept nothing less than the whole family is there, and repentant for their sins."

"If he had one ounce of Christianity in his soul, then he would have come to see us, not you, with his demands."

"You will get all your family, and mine condemned."

"We will see Mother."

Harry arrived at the vicarage a little more than half an hour later. The vicar appeared more receptive to his arguments than his mother-in-law had been, without really revealing anything of what he would say at Sunday service. Or even if he would mention their lapses. He simply said, "I don't know what I am going to say, it is the Almighty who gives me the words."

"Will you be coming to see Faith? I am sure she would be pleased to hear what you have to say."

"It is for her to come to me, Harry."

"But she is ill, she is frightened to go outside and see anyone." He almost added, 'And you could go all the way to Wingfield just to put pressure on us to attend, instead of the more logical coming to see us.'

Harry arrived home in the belief that he had convinced the vicar of his arguments.

The following day Harry, Mary and young Harry were seated, together with the older couple, towards the front of the congregation, directly in the glare of the Reverend Tucker.

Mr Tucker's eyes had run the length of the family when he had begun the sermon. He started mildly enough, expressing his sorrow that a whole family living within the parish had fallen down on their obligations and not kept God's holy day sacrosanct, even saying it was necessary to work on the Sabbath day in pursuit of money. Warming to his theme that God would punish, indeed had already punished, that family, and Jesus himself had said there was no room in the kingdom of God for the unrepentant sinner, the vicar droned on in much the same vein. He even blamed Faith's parents, without mentioning them by name, even intimating that they shouldn't have gone to another church. The argument seemed to be, 'If they were not prepared, or were unable, to walk back to this church, then they shouldn't have left the area'.

Harry smiled inwardly at this.

Then the ordeal was over and the only sound came from the scraping of their Sunday shoes across the gravel as they made their way from St Martin's church. The only words that were spoken by any of them was a good afternoon or two to acquaintances as they trudged back the mile and a half towards the dairy.

It was Mary who first broke the silence, as they approached home, "I didn't like that man very much."

"Then you will quickly have to learn to like him, my girl," her grandmother retorted, "because you will be seeing a lot more of him."

Mary caught her father's eye and didn't say anything else.

When they had taken off their Sunday best Mary immediately relieved Sarah of the job of caring for her mother. Putting her arms around her she said, "Come on Mummy, I will get you something to eat."

"Thank you for looking after her," Harry said to Sarah. "Has she been all right?"

"I don't know, she has just sat there."

"This is ridiculous, she needs a good whipping for the trouble she has caused us," Helen said.

"I hardly think that would help," Harry replied.

"You do realize we will be forced to make this journey every week, or the Reverend Tucker will come to fetch us?"

"You are perfectly entitled to attend whatever church you wish," Harry said. "I am sure the vicar of South Wingfield would agree."

"The Reverend Tucker said... "

"Are you looking forward to a ten mile round trip walk in whatever weather every week? Or can you use the wood cart just to satisfy the vicar of St Martin's?"

"Didn't you listen to his service?"

"I listened. But just to humour me, at least talk to your local vicar, see what he has to say."

"Aren't you wanting us here to see what you are doing?"

"Mother, I am quite happy for you to be here, I was thinking of you, that's all."

"You will get her to church every Sunday, won't you?"

"Just as soon as she is able."

"And Mary?"

"Yes, of course Mother."

Not long afterwards Mary and the two Harrys stood beside the woodman's cart as it set off towards South Wingfield. As the cart turned into Sleetmoor Lane on it's way home, Mary said, "Oh dear, I think we will have some trouble there."

"That isn't the thing to say about your grandparents."

"I am being realistic."

"Do you think it would help if we asked the Reverend Tucker if he could call and see mother?" Young Harry asked.

"I don't think so, do you?" his father replied.

Mary said, "It is going to take mummy a long time to get better and people shouting at her, like that man in church, is only going to make things a lot worse."

"We just might have another problem as well," Harry said, "now that they have seen you at church Mary."

"I don't think so," she replied. "After all, I have got a tutor, and I am eight now so I can leave school soon."

There was a period of silence while everyone considered what should be done, or because no one could see a way out of the dilemma.

Mary said, "I had better go to mummy," and she left, without waiting for anyone to question her further.

Young Harry decided he had better go to prepare tomorrow's work.

His father said, "Well, we have to sort something out before next Sunday."

It was a stroke of divine providence, or possibly sheer good luck, or maybe some knowledge of events, that caused the curate, one Mathew Webb, from the chapel of ease dedicated to St Andrew in Somercotes, to call in that very day.

Somercotes hadn't yet got its own church but the chapel was formally administered by the vicar of Riddings church, through this curate, and was already well on the way to being recognised by the Church of England in its own right.

There were several chapels in the village, Wesleyans and Baptists, and some others, with varying allegiances to other breakaway faiths. None of these would have been given any authority by the dogmatic incumbent of St Martin's in Alfreton. However, a church of his own faith could hardly be decried by the Reverend Tucker.

The appearance of the curate had sown the seeds of an idea into Harry's mind. He was well aware that Faith's parents had been ordered to attend St Martin's, even though they resided in another parish. Somercotes was within the parish of Alfreton, but would the vicar risk a confrontation with the vicar of Riddings? That was always supposing they could get the backing of the curate's boss.

Harry had stood watching the man talking to his son. Then as he prepared to go out of the shop, Harry said, "I have a dilemma vicar."

The man was young, scarcely out of his teens, hoping to make his name in the church. He had turned to face Harry.

"My wife is ill, but she is deeply religious and worries that she is unable to get to church."

"She must make her confessions and as soon as she is able to, return to her devotions."

"Are you able to take confessions vicar?"

"I am on my way to the parish meeting, but I will gladly come back later on, if that is all right."

"That would be appreciated vicar."

The man left the shop.

Now the serious bit would begin. Faith had to see this vicar. Harry well remembered the frosty reception she had given the doctor on his last visit. Mary was the key to preparing Faith's mind to the fact that this was a matter of great importance. He was certain that this boy would come back, though he wasn't quite as certain just how quickly.

Harry went in to find out what mother and daughter were doing. Mary had just set her mother some routine tasks, which wouldn't look good when the curate returned. As soon as was practical Harry got his daughter away so that he could explain the situation to her. He never once considered about how within a matter of days, hours even, he had stopped considering Mary as a child and given her the dominant roll in the relationship. Now he explained just what he had arranged.

"I think it may be a little too soon Daddy."

"It's a matter of great urgency that we do something before the Reverend Tucker tells the whole world what sinners we are again at his next service. Something like that could kill our trade for good."

"Something like this could kill mummy for certain, after what happened last Sunday."

"Only if she knew just what did happen last Sunday."

"She knows, didn't you think granny would tell her? She is almost as bad as that vicar."

"Oh dear. Yes, she will think God will strike us all down in our beds, herself included, for our wickedness."

"And what do you think Daddy?"

"Hopefully not, but who knows how a god thinks?"

"Maybe a vicar doesn't know everything."

"Don't let your granny hear you say things like that, or she will think I have brought you up in sin."

"We have to get back to the job in hand, what to do about this curate. Is he as bad as the vicar?"

"I don't know, Mr Tucker is the only vicar I have known."

"I will have to think about what is best."

"We haven't got long, he might be back any minute."

It was Mary herself who told Faith of the forthcoming visit of the young curate. "He is a sort of young trainee vicar."

It was as if Faith feared the wrath of this man as much as she feared the Divine Creator was here to give His judgement of eternal damnation. She had been sitting on the easy chair, now she pulled a pillow in front of her face and started to let out a soft moaning noise.

Eventually Mary could stand it no longer. After trying to put an arm around her to comfort her, and talking softly as if she was trying to get a baby to sleep, she finally gave up and went to talk to her father.

"You will have to stop that man from coming, it'll kill her for sure."

Harry hurried into the back room. Faith hadn't moved and the unearthly moan was still coming from her huddled form.

"He cannot see her, it will be too much, she will be over the edge and we will lose her." Tears were coming from Mary's eyes.

"Right, I will stop him, I'll make sure that young Harry doesn't let him through the shop. I'll tell him to get me and between us we will not let him through. Now I will have to find something reasonable to tell him." He stood there listening to his wife's misery for a minute longer, before putting an arm around his daughter. "Oh Mary, you shouldn't have to put up with all this, it will have to be my job now, I just didn't know."

"It hasn't been so bad, it's just since that man frightened her to death, him and granny between them."

"Mary," her father said sharply. "it's just how vicars are. They think it's their job to get everybody to the church, any way they can, and keep them there every week. And mummy was brought up to fear God's wrath, that's all."

"And all those people who go there every week and then start swearing on the streets, and fighting, rolling on the ground, and being sick afterwards, and frightening the ladies and children so that they dare not go onto the streets, are they good then?"

"It's not the church, it's the pubs that they go to afterwards, when they drink too much alcohol."

"Why doesn't that vicar tell them not to do it then?"

"I suppose he doesn't like that any more than you do, but he can't stop it."

"Well he isn't doing his job then."

At that moment Faith gave a louder sigh and pulled the pillow closer to her face.

"Go outside Daddy, mummy isn't deaf you know." With that she pushed her father outside the room. "And make sure that man doesn't come in."

Harry gave his son a brief summary of recent events. "We have to stop him getting to her, any idea of what to say?"

Mathew Webb didn't arrive that day, nor did he come the following one either. He had either forgotten, or been warned off by his bosses.

C. 1879

Stables and Cow Houses	**Kitchen** Closet Ash Pit
Chop House	**Yard** **Dairy**
Manure	Site of Well
Pigsty	**Kitchen**
Hen Pen and Lumber	
Stables	**Oven** **Sitting Room**
Store Room	**Bakery** **Stairs**
Formaly Dairy Shop	**Shop** **Parlour**

400 so Yards

C. 1920 - 49

Coke Oven	Coke Heap
Coke Oven	Toilet

Bakery

Yard

Kitchen

Storage

Sitting Room

Storage

Stairs

Cottage

(Mrs Banks)

Shop

Parlour

400 sq Yards

C. 1949 - Now

Converted to gas.
Bakrey extended to
boundary. 1949

Gas Oven

Gas Oven

Bakery

Covered Walkway

Toilets | Toilets

Kitchen

Yard

Sitting Room

Prover

Whrel In Ovens

Storage

Stairs

Shop

Office

Storage

Shutter Door

400 so Yards

Chapter 3

The year was 1889. Henry Rogers, vicar of the church of St James's at Riddings in Derbyshire, was admiring the completely refurbished chancel. The church itself was little more than forty years old, in fact, about the same age as Henry himself.

And it had a spire. The locals hadn't seen another like it, certainly there were none in the area. They were all the normal oblong, cross-shaped buildings that had graced the religious fraternity, it seemed, for ever. Now they had even refurbished it, seeming to Henry as if all his Christmases had come at once.

He had been sent to, and served his apprenticeship in, the far reaches of darkest Africa as a missionary. And he had expected to be forgotten and remain in that capacity until his bones had become brittle and old, or some unknown tropical disease carried him to a premature grave. Just why the powers that be had recalled him to this new church in a tranquil part of rural England, he had no idea, and he wasn't about to question the reasoning too closely.

It wasn't quite as perfect as he had at first imagined. There was plenty of poverty, malnutrition and disease, infant mortality, and bad housing. That seemed the lot of the poor, the world over. In complete contrast with this, there were great leaps forwards, like canals taking the coal and iron towards the industrial centres not dreamt of twenty years ago when, as a young priest, he had left his native shores. There were even great engineering works only four miles away at Butterley, where great forges belched fire into the night sky. Some called it magnificent, others the fires of the devil incarnate. Then there were the huge new roads just being made in his youth, now almost abandoned in favour of the rail networks that were superseding even the canals.

Recently they had made a new water system. Every home had fresh running water coming from taps. This was a wonder to behold. This was all a new world he couldn't even have envisaged when he went away.

He had never remembered the intense cold as he had sweated in the tropical heat. But he was a priest, and it was his duty to serve God wherever he was sent.

It was whilst he was admiring his new chancel that his curate, whose job it was to administer the chapel of ease in the neighbouring parish of Somercotes whilst it waited to be elevated to the title of parish church, approached him.

"Hello sir", the curate began, "I wanted your advice on a little matter." He immediately explained about the predicament with Faith Kane, and her brush with the domineering Reverend Tucker of Alfreton. "Nominally Somercotes is within the district of Riddings, and Mr Tucker is no longer responsible for the spiritual welfare of anyone in the Somercotes parish."

"Tell him then, what is the problem?"

"Mr Tucker is a formidable man, he even went to admonish her parents who also reside in another parish, that of South Wingfield, which isn't, and never was, within Alfreton's jurisdiction."

"I see. Have you formed an impression of this Faith Kane, because you seem to have formed one of Mr Tucker? Why doesn't she just go to church, it is her religious duty?"

"Mrs Kane is apparently ill, and frightened to go anywhere."

"I still don't quite see what you want me to do."

"I would like you to just talk to Mrs Kane, and then tell me what I should do."

Henry Rogers stood for a minute, a smile playing in the corner of his eyes. "They call it the melancholia," he said. "I saw a witch doctor cure a woman once with a pile of bones, the most remarkable thing I ever saw."

The curate was shocked. "That is the devil's work, sir."

"I don't think the villagers saw it that way, and surely if she was cured then it was the will of God. And remember, Christ himself did some miraculous things, he cured the sick, he fed the five thousand with a few loaves and fishes, he even raised the dead. I wonder just how the people of his day, saw this. Did they think it the devil's work?" The young man had gone a deathly white.

Henry Rogers either didn't notice, or chose to ignore it. "Come on lad, we will go and see your Mrs Kane."

"What, now?"

"No time like the present. And if I understand correctly, your Reverend Tucker will probably give another of his vitriolic sermons on Sunday, that is if we don't forestall him."

So it was, and without any more prompting, that the man of the cloth, with his young assistant almost trotting behind to keep up, went for a little more than a mile along the old Greenhill track and arrived at *Joseph's.*

Henry Rogers was about to enter through the baker's shop when his curate indicated the next door, into the dairy. It was young Harry who was inside the shop, he looked startled as he saw the young, breathless curate, with the taller, greying priest with those twinkling eyes.

"Is it your mother that we are here to see lad?"

"Er, I suppose so."

"Show us through then."

The curate added, "This is my boss the Reverend Henry Rogers of Riddings."

The older Harry now stood behind him, wishing he could have had the chance to at least talk to him before they saw his wife. But this priest clearly was in no mood for delay, so with no option he led them into the back room.

Faith looked up. She was seated on the easy chair and suddenly terrified by the prospect of another priest. Mary, who was by her side, also feared another Tucker-style tirade, and the effect it would have on her mother. The drapes were covering the windows to keep out what light there was and Mary, at least, wanted them to remain there if at all possible.

The young curate was fearful of some devil's medicine, and the only calming figure in the room was Henry Rogers himself.

He took hold of both of Faith's hands in his own and felt the trembling woman's fingers.

"Come my child, it is not so bad as you think, we will soon have you around again." He stood holding her hands with the crowd of interested spectators watching his every move from their own different perspectives.

Henry Rogers looked back on the gathered host, then said, "I think we should have a quiet little talk, all on our own, don't you Faith? You don't mind me calling you Faith do you?"

"No vicar." She spoke in a timid, frightened little girl's voice.

He stood up, still holding her hands.

"Right, if there is no objection, Faith and I will have our little talk, whilst you all wait outside. Please close the door, if you don't mind."

The door closed behind them.

Still holding her hands, the vicar continued, "You have got yourself into quite a mess for nothing, you know."

"The Reverend Tucker said God... "

"Let's forget what the Reverend Tucker said, for now."

"But... "

"No buts. Have you heard the parable of the prodigal son who wasted his share of the father's wealth, but his father killed the fatted calf and had a party because he had come home?"

"But that is something different."

"Your father in heaven simply wants you back in the fold."

"I can't, the Rev... "

"I thought we agreed to forget anyone else. You do want to be welcomed back into church don't you?"

"Yes Father."

"Then that is all that matters. Now, close your eyes, stand up and put your hands on my shoulders." Next he rambled on, in what she thought must be in Latin. She felt his hands holding her head firmly and his calm reassuring voice, in English now, say firmly, "Take away all doubts, bring our sister back into your house, Father."

Gradually the trembling ceased, she felt calmer now, as if the cares of the world had lifted from her mind. She felt his hands relax and then opened her eyes, looking straight into the twinkling brown eyes of the priest.

"How are you Faith?"

"I feel very weak, but I think I am all right."

The man smiled and sat down beside her.

"It's been quite an ordeal you have had Faith, but you must attend church this week. It might be better if you went somewhere different than Mr Tucker's church, at least until you feel completely well."

"I would like to go to your church, if I can vicar."

"It would be my privilege Faith."

They sat side by side a little while longer and he still held her hand. His voice, when he eventually spoke was quiet, calming, almost matter-of-fact, "I think you are all right now, don't you Faith?"

She looked into those twinkling eyes. "I didn't know there were any priests like you vicar, I thought they were all like… "

He held up his hand to silence her. "We agreed you wouldn't mention that name."

She was smiling now. "I'm sorry."

Henry Rogers' face was wreathed in smiles as he stood up and pushed open the door.

The gathered crowd traipsed in. Mary was first, she rushed and put her arms around her mother. "Are you all right Mummy?" her voice mirroring her concern. But Faith's smile seemed little short of a miracle.

"What's happened?" Harry asked.

"There are more things happen in heaven and hell than we ever really understand Harry. Suffice to say God's will, not ours, will prevail in the long run."

Harry Kane's face was totally bemused.

But Henry Rogers had no doubt, as he added softly, "Have faith my son." His smile confirmed something had happened. "I simply asked if Faith would prefer to go to a different church until she gets a little stronger. She has been very ill you know."

"Has… been… ill?"

"Oh, I think the worst is behind her."

The vicar left the house, his curate behind him.

"I'll see you on Sunday," Faith called after him, but he was already on his way.

As soon as they were out of earshot the curate said, "Just what happened in there?"

"Oh, nothing really. She was just a little frightened of Alfreton's priest, so she asked if she could come to St James's on Sunday."

"Just like that?"

"It isn't what happened, or what didn't happen, it is simply what she believes."

On the Sunday, a clear, crisp, sunny day, Henry Rogers stood seemingly without a care in the world as he greeted his congregation by the doorway. It was as if he had never thought of Faith since their one and only meeting. Now, as she entered the church flanked by her family, Henry briefly touched her hand with not the slightest hint of recognition, and soon the service was underway.

Harry thought it must be part of the treatment to ignore what had previously occurred.

Henry Rogers told of his time in Africa, of the little black people anxious for the word of the Lord that he had taken to them. "They didn't have a fine new church like the people of Riddings. They sat on a grassy bank, but there was fulfilment in their eyes as they received the word of God. It was an uplifting time for me as much as for them. Remember, there is more joy in the giver than the receiver, and I gained as much if not more than them. I was able to bring them all the glory of God," he concluded, "but they gave me so much more, their sheer happiness as they found God's kingdom.

"Now I would like to tell you another story, of a very remarkably brave lady. She was lost and alone, believing herself outside of God's holy kingdom, then God smiled on her, and she knew all was well again. She was told of the mercy of the Lord and today, for the first time in a long time, she sits here in this church with God's light shining on her. Would you mind standing up Faith?"

Harry and Mary looked at one another. Was everything that had been accomplished going to vanish in a single instance because this priest had not given it a little more time?

But Faith stood up.

There was a ripple of applause until it built to a crescendo.

Mary looked up at her father, then her mother, there was an emotion approaching terror in her young eyes, but she need not have worried. The tears in Faith's eyes were of pure joy.

Someone else was closely watching the events, and the curate didn't quite see it in the same way. He was thinking of the witch doctor in darkest Africa with his pile of bones.

It so happened that the bishop had visited that day, mainly to see the renovations to the chancel. He had congratulated the Reverend Henry Rogers on the full congregation and on his inspiring service, before the curate had the opportunity the have a word. Having approached the eminent churchman when he was out of earshot of anyone else, he asked permission to speak.

"Go on lad, just what is troubling you?"

"Well sir, I am worried at the way Mr Rogers got that woman back into church."

"In what way is that wrong?"

"He talked about witch doctors in Africa, with bones and mumbo-jumbo, and he said whatever way he could get her back would be all right. This is surely the way of the devil."

"Was it these bones that changed her then?"

"He didn't actually take any bones, but he would have consorted with the devil to ingratiate himself in your eyes."

"I will have a quiet word with Mr Rogers, but in the meantime I would advise you to concentrate on getting your own parish up and running. It isn't good to have disputes within the church."

"Of course not sir, but I thought you should know."

"Certainly."

Whether his eminence the bishop ever spoke to the Reverend Henry Rogers is not recorded. But it is certain the curate continued to regard what had happened as something quite outside his own understanding.

Harry Kane's family certainly talked about the Reverend Rogers as though he were some miracle worker. Mary, now nine years old, walked all the way to Riddings church to thank him for giving her mummy back.

One day the family, that is Harry, Faith and Mary, but not young Harry because someone had to remain in charge of the dairy, walked the five miles to her mother's house to thank her for coming that day. It is known that Mr Tucker gave another of his venomous sermons the following Sunday, but that none of the family were there to listen. It was noticeable that in the next few months his own congregation began to decline, but that of Riddings was always full to capacity, and that the Reverend Henry Rogers began to have the reputation of something of a faith healer.

At nine years of age Mary had now no need of further education so they had to let Sarah go. She had expected this anyway. She always spoke well of the Kanes, and the education she had from young Mary stood her in good stead for the rest of her life.

It was several month later that John Sergeant was standing outside his shop, when a runaway horse and carriage ran straight into him, dragging him along the street. When his mangled, blood-soaked body was disentangled from under the wheels, it was Mary who tended to his wounds and made him as comfortable as possible. The doctor said there was nothing else that could be done.

It was doubtful if he ever realised what had happened to him. But Mary had a natural tendency as a carer and at first it seemed as if John would be up and about. But then he became more and more lethargic, the doctor said he must have contracted a virus, and after several relapses he became so weak everyone eventually gave up hope.

The new vicar of Somercotes read the last rites, but it wasn't the curate Mathew Webb who had succeeded to the post. The bishop had seen fit to appoint another, one Sebastian Smith.

Now it was Mary, still only nine years old, who became the sole baker. She was up by four each morning to knead the dough and bake the bread. It just seemed natural that eventually Mary took over entirely when John, after yet another relapse, completely expectedly, suddenly died. He was interred at Riddings church on a miserably rainy day in October of the year 1892.

Dorothy Sergeant never returned, so that was one mystery that was not resolved.

With no one clamouring for the result of Joseph Carlin's will, there was no further mention of it. So whether it was ever read, or what was in the document, or what happened to his house in Newark, none of the locals ever knew.

So it was the Kanes who carried on blissfully, until eventually Mary fell in love and got married to the son of the flour miller on Sleetmoor Lane, in the year 1897.

Young Harry took ill the year before, it was said to be cholera. It was odd though, because with the advent of the clean running water, the disease, once rampant in the area, had seemed to have totally vanished locally.

Everyone knew it was incurable. He went to a sanatorium but it only delayed the inevitable. Both of his parents took it hard and their own end followed not long afterwards.

Faith's parents seemed as robust as ever, they looked as if they would last for ever.

Joe Dawes, himself a farmer of the former reclaimed common land and grandson of the landowner Job Dawes who had lain claim to the property almost fifty years earlier, now took over abstract of title with his cousin Josiah Whyler as the baker. He expanded the bakery so that the stables, which was a far larger building, now housed the bakery.

Josiah seemed at first to have been a very ambitious man and borrowed heavily to expand the trade. He married Isabella Duncan, an empty-headed local girl who had at first dazzled him with her flashy appearance, and with his new bride took up residence in the main house behind the shop and bakery. His wife was the sort who painted her face with the latest cosmetics and wore enough jewellery to grace a duchess entertaining in a great mansion. That may have been all right in the dance halls of London or Paris, but seemed totally out of place in a country village. She also had a taste for the latest drapes and furniture, and spoke glibly of altering the whole place so that she could show off to her friends.

"I could have horses in the back place, it had once housed horses anyway," she said.

"No, they were working animals, used to deliver the bread, not something to impress your cronies, you know," Josiah said. "Something to earn cash, not to throw it away so you can look something you are definitely not. It also might have escaped your notice that the old stables is now the bakery."

"The bakery could go where the dairy used to be."

"Didn't you listen to a word I said? If you want to spend money you have to knuckle down and earn it. And besides, just who would ride these animals if you had them? You can't, can you, and even more important, who would clean them out every day? I haven't noticed you getting down to cleaning anything a great deal."

She was prattling on and it was doubtful if she had listened to anything Josiah had said. She lived in this little dream world of her own.

Something had to happen and it did.

For a start Josiah turned the dairy into a house and let it to a local couple. So it was certain the bakery couldn't go there. Isabella still talked of her grand schemes. Couldn't that woman ever be practical?

Then one day Josiah was in the shop serving a new customer when Isabella flounced through.

"God, what was that?" he asked. "She looks like a real Jezebel."

"Yes she is a bit over the top," Josiah agreed.

It was the first time he had realized what an impression she made on others, and there and then decided he must do something about it. But what? For the rest of that day he mused on the problem.

He knew others had run this place very successfully. Harry Kane had all his family knuckling down and working at it, and Joseph Carlin whose name had become a byword in the local folklore. He had been the thing everyone aspired to be, a gentleman.

None of these had a millstone like Isabella. What should he do? The first thought was drown her; he smiled at the thought, but it wasn't really practical.

His mind was on Harry Kane again. He had heard the story of Harry and Faith, of how she had lost her marbles and Harry had taken her to see that vicar at Riddings church, the one who performed miracles. She had never been crazy again. The story went that he had learned it from some witch doctor with a pile of old bones, in the jungles of Africa.

Isabella was sort of crazy too. It wasn't natural to spend a lifetime painting your face. God, what did she think she was?

Now, Josiah had never been a particularly religious man, but the more he thought of it, the better it all seemed. He would go and see the Reverend Henry Rogers the vicar of Riddings. As far as he knew he was still there.

What would he say? The first thing was to make sure he was there, then he would try to have a word.

The following afternoon he made his way to Riddings and he was standing outside the impressive church reading the noticeboard. Yes, it still listed the Reverend Henry Rogers as the resident vicar. That at least, was promising.

As he was reading the board, the young vicar who passed by was surely not the man he wanted.

"Excuse me sir, I see Mr Rogers is listed as the vicar."

"Yes."

"I wondered where I might find him."

"Well, this Sunday he will be attending a conference, where he is expected to speak. I believe the following week he will be back in his pulpit."

"Oh." Josiah was clearly disappointed.

"I trust you will be attending the Sunday services in the same way as if Mr Rogers were there young man."

"I normally attend Somercotes church sir, but I just wished to have a quiet word with the Reverend Rogers, if that was possible vicar."

"If you wish to make a confession, I will gladly give you a little of my time my son."

(The fact that he called him 'my son' annoyed Josiah but he gave no sign.)

"No sir, it is nothing like that vicar."

"Then just why do you wish to see him?"

Why do these people always seem to talk down to everyone, thought Josiah. He turned away, saying, "I will come back next week sir." And before the man could question his further, he was on his way.

This was good really. It would give him a little more time to formulate what he was going to say.

During the next ten days, before the expected return of this supposed miracle worker, Josiah was in a remarkably good mood, convinced in his own mind that his problems would soon be solved. Then on the day he intended to go to Riddings, he felt surprisingly nervous. The more he considered his predicament, the less sense it made. It seemed ludicrous to ask for help from a vicar, simply because his wife decorated her face, and wore heaps of jewellery. A man was expected to control his family.

He had almost decided not to go when Isabella flounced past him. The more he saw her now, the more embarrassed he became.

So, dressed in his best bib and tucker, he joined the congregation at the church of St James's at Riddings.

It was the fourteenth of January in the last year of the century. News had come in of a great battle at Rorke's Drift in the Zulu wars, although this had taken place some twenty years before. (Events took their time to reach backwaters such as this.) The Reverend Rogers took this as his theme, decrying the fact of the loss of life. And drawing on his own adventures in that dark continent, he warmed to his theory that it should be the missionary not the soldier who ventured to these far corners of the empire.

"In the final analysis it will have to be the church that brings the word of God to these peoples, and our task will be so much harder now," he concluded.

Josiah together with the rest of the congregation was inspired by his rousing words, but the rest of the service seemed so much mumbo–jumbo to him.

Then came the end and the people were filing out into the crisp, cold, sunny daylight. Josiah hung back to be the last person to emerge. The Reverend Rogers was shaking each hand in turn and Josiah almost chickened out of his self-appointed task.

He noticed the twinkling eyes first.

"Hello, is this your first time at our church? It is a fine building don't you think?"

"Er, yes." The man hadn't called him 'son', he thought.

He was loitering.

"I think there is something you wanted."

"How did you know?"

"You waited to be the last out, you are new here, and you seem as if you want to say something."

Those eyes were still twinkling, as if they were laughing at him.

"I'm from the bakery in Somercotes and a long time ago you helped Faith Kane, people still talk about it," he blurted out.

"It's very kind of you to say so, but that wasn't the way it was. Faith was ill, she needed a little reassurance that's all there was to it."

"My wife is kind of ill too. Well, she is not exactly ill, but I don't know quite how to put it."

"Shall we go inside and have a little talk about it?"

He led Josiah into a little side room inside the church and once he was comfortably seated said, "Shall we start by you telling me who you are, and just what ails your wife?"

"My name is Josiah Whyler and I now run the bakery in Somercotes sir. My wife Isabella is making a laughing stock of me. She paints her face and wears a lot of trinkets, and I have heard people calling her a Jezebel. She won't help me to run the place and just wants to throw money away on ridiculous things just to impress her cronies, and we simply haven't got it."

"Surely you have spoken to her about this."

"She ignores me and does it all the more."

Now he had put it all into words he felt a little foolish. The vicar couldn't do anything anyway.

The Reverend Henry Rogers remained silent.

Josiah said, "I'm sorry, it was a silly idea coming to see you anyway, it's my problem and I shouldn't have bothered you with it."

"Sometimes it does good just to put it into words, share the problem, then it often doesn't seem so bad."

"Yes I suppose so."

"Perhaps if she had someone else who depended on her, someone helpless."

"You mean a baby?"

"Some people completely change with that sort of responsibility."

"We have been together for above a year and a half, and nothing has happened yet."

"You will have to learn to be patient, these things don't always happen when we want them to, it is God's will."

Josiah stood up. He was beginning to feel more than just a little foolish.

"I will pray for you."

"Thank you," he was backing to the door, he just wanted to be as far from here as he could, this had been a daft idea anyway.

Isabella was standing near the door when he got back to the bakery, a demanding, confrontational expression on her face. Her face seemed even more painted, and there were more gaudy ornaments dangling around her than usual. Or was that just his imagination?

"Where do you think you have been dressed in your Sunday best?"

Josiah was normally in his work clothes.

"If you really want to know, I have been to church to see the reverend Rogers."

"Why?" The smile was no more than a frozen grimace on her face. "You have never wanted to go to church as long as I have known you."

Stung by her attitude he snapped back, "I wanted to now, so that I could find out just what I should do to rid myself of a Jezebel."

"He's the man who has the bones like a witch doctor, who cures people who are ill, or daft, probably kills them as well, for all I know."

The smile on her face was still there, but it seemed frozen, as though it was a death mask.

"Well, we shall see, won't we."

"What did he say?" She looked shaken, far more so than he would have expected.

"That he would pray, nothing more."

Wherever she had intended to go that night, she didn't, just standing outside for a while before coming quietly inside.

Josiah went to bed early because he needed to be up early to prepare the bread doughs.

He used the old sponge method of mixing; a dough to stand, then mixing some of this into every later mix. This gave it lift, in the same way that later generations would use yeast.

Many bakers at the time put their dough outside to get yeast spores from the atmosphere, which was a more haphazard method and, of course, they would mix whatever was wind-borne into their finished products. Another disadvantage was during winter cold the dough wouldn't rise at all.

It was John Sergeant who had perfected the idea of saving some old dough, and he had never been frightened of the winter's cold.

Now, when Josiah went to bed he was surprised to find Isabella already there.

After a little silence she said timidly, "I didn't know you wanted to get rid of me."

"I don't."

"But you went to that witch doctor, and told him I was a Jezebel."

"No, but I did say you painted yourself up, you wanted to spend all the money, even that we hadn't earned yet, and that you didn't help around the place."

"I thought you liked me as I was, I was like this when we married."

"But you seem to flaunt yourself."

"You aren't jealous surely?"

"No, not really, but I don't like to hear people calling you behind your back, and me too."

"Did you ask that man to get rid of me?"

"Of course not."

She was quiet for a few minutes, and he said, "Go to sleep, it'll soon be time for me to get up."

Isabella still painted her face, but it was noticeably less 'over the top', and she did do a little to help around the place. Not much mind, but it was an improvement from Josiah's point of view. There was no more talk of horses, or any such ideas, and the following year she presented Josiah with a bouncing baby girl. The birth had been long and traumatic, but Isabella bore it with fortitude.

The tale of his visit to the 'witch doctor' soon got around the village, and it further enhanced the Reverend Rogers' reputation.

A short time after the birth Josiah suggested they visited Riddings church and thanked the vicar. Rather surprisingly Isabella thought this was a good idea. "It will show him I am a good wife now," she said. Then as an afterthought she added, "Did he really have a pile of bones?"

Josiah smiled. "No, of course not, we just had a little talk, that's all."

They did go, but once more Mr Rogers was visiting another church, he seemed to be something of a celebrity these days. They didn't actually go inside, once they found it was a different vicar.

Neither Josiah nor Isabella was in any way religious and as Josiah said, "I couldn't understand what they were babbling about last time." They did say they would go again, but they never did.

The bakery seemed to have been reasonably successful, and they were still there in the year 1906.

In that year Henry Beach bought some lands from Mr Dawes, including a row of property along Leabrooks Road which included the bakery. He therefore became Josiah's landlord.

Henry seemed to have been a farmer, collier and wheeler-dealer, dabbling in whatever was available to support his family of ten kids and, if possible, lift them out of the national malaise of poverty.

Rumours of war were becoming increasingly louder until eventually the assassination of Archduke Franz Ferdinand in Sarajevo precipitated the start of the Great War in 1914.

Josiah was at the bakery at the time Henry purchased the place, and he most likely was still there until the start of the war. Afterwards he certainly was not. Perhaps he went away to fight for king and country, in a false burst of patriotism, which governments always totally forget at the end of hostilities.

Henry had little use for the property and when his son William, still only twenty, returned from the war and expected to resume on the family farm, but by now younger family members did his job, Henry suggested that he should go somewhere to learn the trade of baker. Then he could have a ready-made bakery business. The difficulty appeared to be that there was no business and the property was rapidly becoming a ruin.

He had to repair his property, in between trying to make a living, and the rent would be the going rate, as though the place was in good repair.

What had once been the dairy had been converted into a cottage and there was now a tenant, though if it was dad or granddad who collected the rent, I have no idea. But I strongly suspect it would have been Henry. All in all, Henry didn't appear to be doing his son any favours.

Dad acquired his knowledge elsewhere, and with his new skills began his trade of baker.

There wasn't any electrics. It seemed that Alfreton's council had turned down offers to lay the cables into the town as far back as 1906, in spite of complaining bitterly of being robbed by the gas companies. Threats by the electrical people to force them to comply only hardened their resolve to resist. Most similar sized towns were equipped, or being equipped, with an adequate supply long before the local councillors were dragged kicking and screaming into the modern era.

The locals had to manage with the kerosene lamps with a naked flame inside a bottle to supply their home lighting. And the old lamplighter with his flame on a pole to light the streetlamps, was an innovation many other councils had already scrapped long ago.

George Kenning came round on his horse and dray selling the kerosene, mainly extracted from the Riddings well. The same Kenning who would later make his fortune from a franchise as sole seller of Morris cars throughout the Midlands. This was the franchise turned down by garage owner Charlie Argile, who said to me on one occasion, long ago, "Well, who would have thought those things would ever have caught on."

Not to be caught out with the disadvantage of no electricity, my father William rigged up his own generator on the floor above the bakery, with an elaborate system of belts coming down through the ceiling and a wooden lever to select which machine it would power. It must have been something he had learned whilst in the forces. This 'Heath Robinson' system would work perfectly for the next forty years until the belated arrival of the national grid and connection to that supply.

He also had a van, as opposed to the horse and dray which was the norm.

From necessity he had to climb onto the roof and apparently made a good enough job of the repairs so that no other work would be needed for years.

William, my dad, was as well equipped, and certainly as progressive, as his money allowed. The future seemed as reasonably secure as any could be, in an age of little certainty.

In this world of ours things never quite work out as planned.

The obvious advantage he enjoyed over his rivals was of course only transitory, until the event of the council relenting and the national grid with its power supply becoming readily available.

Dad was always innovative, for instance we were among the first to have a telephone locally, reflected with its number of 'Somercotes 3'. Certainly this was before the local doctor.

I remember people used to phone the bakery with their illnesses and I, as a kid, or someone out of the bakery, used to have to run across the road to the local surgery with a scrap of paper to alert the doctor.

We had taken to using the kitchen, which was situated behind the house and in front of the bakery, as our main living room. We had the open fires in both the house and the kitchen, but this room was always warmer during the winter and pleasantly cooler in the warmest of summer days. No one had ever questioned the reason. Then one day dad decided we would take up the flagstones which were becoming worn, and make it even more presentable. It was going to be covered with some nice tiles.

We were in for a shock. Just under the floor was a huge well, still full of water. Some of the flagstones had worn unbelievably thin and it seemed only divine providence that had forestalled a calamity.

After taking all relevant advice, and seemingly every official from everywhere gazing into its depth and samples being taken to analyse its purity (but for what earthly reason?), we had a row of lorries filled with rubble to end any use it could ever have.

Throughout this period the front, left-hand side of the property, which had been the dairy and had graduated into being the cottage, had an occupant. During the period of my youth it had always been Lemual, and I believe it was Emily, Banks who lived there. She was bedfast and the bed had been brought downstairs. She was very demanding and had a loud voice. I always remember hearing her shouting, "Lemual do this!" or "Do that!" Then one day he had simply got on a bus and gone all the way to Nottingham, which was at least an hour's bus journey, then got on a tram and gone to Trent Bridge. Once there, presumably unable to stand the incessant demanding of his wife, he had climbed onto the parapet and jumped in. The coroner said it was suicide while the balance of his mind was disturbed. But how odd it seemed, to travel all that way and do that. It all seemed very strange. The next day after the event dad had come in from his round and said, "You will never guess who I have seen. Emily Banks striding it out, on her way returning from Alfreton."

"She can't be, she doesn't ever get out of bed," I said.

Dad always saw the good it everyone. He said, "It's the shock, it can do some strange things to people."

Her story had been that her parents had always had money and her mother had died young. Her father had remarried a dolly bird, no older than his daughter. Anyway, he had left his wealth to his wife and then, on her demise, the residue would pass to his only daughter Emily. Well, just after Lemual's suicide she inherited what was left of the family money. Now she returned to her former helpless state, with a nephew looking after her. He openly said, "I've had about enough of this. If she doesn't die soon, I will be long gone."

Well, she passed away eventually and presumably the nephew got what he considered his just deserts, and I hope he enjoyed his fortune.

I remember hearing people say, "Fancy her living in that little cottage and she had all that money."

But the truth was she never had any money, not until it was far too late for it to do her any good. I don't know how much money it actually was, but I don't suppose it was that much.

The way that things work out is always strange.

Well, after Mrs Banks died dad didn't relet the cottage. It reverted to storerooms and the bakery expanded so that the whole of the property was now the bakery. We had been desperately short of room and we now had more room to breathe, as it were.

Just after the war the scientists were working on a new system of making bread, and for some strange reason this was on the government's official secrets list. Trade journals hinted that something was going on, all very hush-hush. Eventually dad decided to write directly to the research place in Chorleywood for any information that might be available. After all, this could conceivably affect our whole future. A brief acknowledging note told us that we would be contacted by the machine manufacturers in due course.

So it was that the reply eventually came, not from the research people, but from two different machine makers, one in Wales and one in Lancashire.

The Lancashire people said they would keep us in touch with any future development.

We were far longer hearing from the other people. Then, one day out of the blue, there arrived a machine, a square box. This had come from the Welsh machine men. My father was soon on the phone, we hadn't asked for a machine, only for information.

Our normal machines mixed one and a half 140lb bags of flour into the mixer at a go. The method was: a mix for about twenty-five minutes, pull that bowl away and let stand. Another 260 loaf mix, then a third, then the first was again put into the mixer for a remix, this would stand for about twenty minutes. After a further recovery period this was then fed into the machine for dividing, moulding and tinning. It was proved (left to rise) then baked, perhaps getting our first bread some three and a half hours after the original mix.

This square mixing-box, with no connection to our normal methods, seemed at the least bizarre. The machine men had sent their own operatives and they would show us how it worked.

It would make fifty loaves and in three minutes we would have the first dough, saving almost two hours and doing away with the need for those heavy mixing bowls.

In another three minutes we then had another fifty loaves and by the time we had loaded the dividers and moulders, the next lot was following on.

Another advantage was we could use home-grown, weaker flour and get top class results. So we were buying cheaper, but more tasty grades of flour. Also, instead of five men on the night shift, we could manage with four working for less hours.

Furthermore, to allay any doubts, we needed to pay nothing until we were completely sure. This would be the first one they had ever installed.

Once more we had a decided advantage over our rivals.

I remember some eighteen months afterwards, going to look around one of these multi-national bakeries and being told by their head spokesman that they had just installed another of these high-speed machines. It was bigger of course, but shared the same principles. "This is the latest innovation. All the small firms will be unable to compete, they will all have to buy from us, or they will be forced to close down."

It gave me a lot of pleasure to reply, "We have been in possession of, and using this principle for the last eighteen months."

Once more dad had trusted his own instinct in the innovation stakes.

We had solar panels on the bakery roof a little after the war, the first I had ever seen, but this time, it didn't work quite so well. Although we had as much hot water as we wanted, the first time we needed any maintenance the firm had gone out of business and no one seemed to understand the principles of the thing. Someone told me years afterwards that the thing had been wired backwards, and it could have had twice the efficiency. But then, you don't always win. I bet if dad had realized he would had been sorting it out.

My Story (Chapter 1)

It was perhaps inevitable that, sooner or later, we should have come across this place. Just a group of lads who went to different dances every Saturday night in my dad's bread van. We had been doing this for the last year, since I had finished my obligatory two-year stint of army national service.

The Sundays of the nineteen fifties was different to today. There were no dances on Sundays, the law, petty restrictions, something anyway, and it wasn't allowed.

Somehow we found this place, it was basically the clubhouse of a lido, and there was music, singing, dancing, drinking, and it was Sunday, just perfect.

We had walked over to the bar, then with the inevitable drinks in our hands had turned to study the talent. A girl was singing and I turned towards the stage as my friends wandered away from the bar. The spotlight was picking up the highlights in her shoulder-length, jet-black hair. Her skin was brown like a perfect suntan, and those big brown eyes were looking towards the entwined bodies swaying on the dance floor. Her voice filled the room with rhythmic melodies, and in my imagination it was the way an angel must enrapture the gods in the heavens of some Greek mythology.

I looked around, people were dancing, talking, doing normal things. Wasn't anyone else captivated by this paragon of beauty? I turned towards a man who just happened to be standing next to me at the bar.

"Who is the girl?" I asked.

"That's Millie," he replied, and then, after what appeared to be an age, he added, "my wife."

"Oh, I'm sorry, I didn't know." I was instantly back down to an earthly reality. And he, sensing the confusion in me, just smiled, like a man who had seen it all so many times before.

"It's all right," he said, "she has that effect on some men."

His words seemed like a sudden dousing from a bucket of cold water, ending all ideas of a heavenly fulfilment.

I asked him if he would like a drink, and bought him one.

Millie was singing again. I tried to drag my eyes away from her captivating virtues, feigning indifference, or at least no more than polite interest. Eventually she left the stage and was coming towards us, or more correctly towards her husband, who just happened to be talking to me.

"Would you mind if I asked her to dance," I asked, as she walked towards us.

"She is her own woman, it is her you have to ask, not me," came back the reply.

We all talked, about something, or nothing, then when it looked as if the she might be preparing to go and sing again, I asked, "Would you like a dance?"

She was in my arms, gliding with a natural rhythm, but I was good too. I'd had some professional training and had honed my skills with scores of different girls in dozens of different venues. From tangos and waltzes to jiving and jitterbugs, I could take centre stage with the best. And Millie was the best.

She didn't sing any more that night.

Suddenly as I took her back towards her husband, I was conscious of the amount of time we had spent together on the dance floor.

"I hope he doesn't mind," I said.

She smiled. "Oh, it'll be all right."

Too soon that night came to an end. She was walking home with a crowd including her husband, towards the village which was about half a mile away. I was driving past them with my friends, maybe it was the one and only time I would ever see her. A last lingering glance at them, she didn't appear to notice me, and we had passed and vanished into the night.

I didn't know then, and she would never know, but that girl would, in one way or another control my whole life.

The next Sunday night I had dropped my friends and was alone at the lido. Again we danced, under the benevolent gaze of her husband. His name, I had learned, was Al. She did sing, a little, but mainly we danced.

The third Sunday Al was working. He drove coaches and had gone to the coast. At the end of the night I offered to drive her back to the village, but she said she had come with a group of girls and it would be better if she went back with them.

The following week she told me of some event in Nottingham, and wondered if I would like to take her there. It was tempting, but I voiced my doubts, "I don't think Al would approve of that."

"It's his idea," she replied.

I looked, obviously, somewhat sceptically and she continued,

"He wants you to come to see him, before you go home, and talk about it."

By this time I knew the couple's story.

They were South African by birth, and the South Africa of the fifties with its dreaded apartheid separation system forbade mixed colour marriages. Al was white, a descendent from the Dutch ruling class known as the Boers. Both Millie's parents were white. Her father was of German decent, and her mother a white Filipino. Her brother and two sisters were also white, but Millie was a throwback to some Spanish forebear. She had bred exactly to the principles described by Gregor Mendel the Austrian monk/biologist who demonstrated it would always be the fourth child who carried the genes.

People were classed as either black, white or Cape Coloured. Millie was classed as Cape Coloured and must have been an embarrassment to a family who embraced the whole system of the superior white race. She was excluded from many of the privileges of her family.

Her father died young as the result of a tragic accident and her mother never remarried. But she did appear to have thrown herself into a whirl of social events such as partying etc. when the little brown-skinned girl was carefully kept from view.

Millie was, however, blossoming into this incredible beauty, but the colour thing meant that she would eventually and inevitably be attached to the Cape Coloured group and spend her future among them.

A tall, good-looking white man, some six years her senior, had other ideas and it wasn't long before he made his intention known. Al wanted her and was prepared to go to any length to have her. His proposal of marriage, though probably seeming a gift from heaven to her mother, was of course against the apartheid code and wouldn't be allowed by the State.

Another snag, from his point of view, was that Millie wasn't at all keen on the idea. But at least there wasn't any objection from either family, if some way could be found to validate the union.

Eventually Al hit on the idea of continuing his studies in an English university, where the marriage would be acceptable, and eventually, no doubt with the connivance of others, Millie agreed to the union.

All too soon a whole new life was opening up and the newlyweds were on board ship and bound for England, where Al would begin his studies at Nottingham University. Millie would be the breadwinner. But like many another well laid plan, it was doomed to failure when Millie became pregnant on her way to her new life.

They landed on a foggy day, directly contrasting with the near perfect weather of their homeland and, in her mind at least, there was a sense of foreboding for the future. All thoughts of the university education, with its bright prospects, were now put on hold. The world of the mid-fifties, with the aftermath of the war, the disillusionment and the drabness all too recent a memory, the low wages and grinding poverty was something the couple hadn't experienced before. Al continually turned down all offers of financial help from his family, saying they were all right, and insisting privately to Millie, "I am determined to show them we can do it on our own."

He obtained a succession of humdrum jobs and they lived in rented rooms until they eventually managed to buy a caravan.

Millie, now with a second child, earned money as a model. Photographs, sympathetically done in bathing costumes or nighties, were on calendars, mostly abroad, and proved a nice if only occasional earner.

In the mid-fifties more money could be earned if girls would pose topless, which was the new innovation of the time. Millie politely declined. "I wouldn't have liked that" she said.

Still, she earned some fifty or sixty pounds for several hours photo shoot, when the average weekly wage for the working class was probably about twelve pounds a week. And then as the pictures were accepted for calendars other welcome cheques of a similar amount would come through the post. "They were for treats," she said.

Al worked all the hours that he could. Any additional trips to the coast at weekends helped, and with the tips added they proved very acceptable. Because of this, Millie was left at home alone with the kids many weekends.

So Al came up with this solution. He explained it to me on that night I went to see him.

"Millie needs the stimulation of going out, the singing, the company. She is a different person than when she stays home with the kids all the time. Oh yes, she's efficient, everything she does is perfect, but somehow she isn't really alive. I don't mind her going out, really I don't. The only thing is, providing she gets someone to look after the kids until I get home, she can go out any night. It might be better if you picked her up somewhere away from here," he continued, "people will be bound to talk. I will simply say you are a friend of the family, but even so, better not to give them too much ammunition."

I didn't consider the logic too closely, I wanted to be with her, to dance, to be there when she sang, and to know that when she came off the stage it would be to me.

Later I would hear another explanation for Al's altruistic attitude. When he made his trips to the coast, a young lady specifically asked for him, and the two of them were often seen walking hand in hand along the sands.

"It doesn't mean anything," Al had protested, "we are just friends. I can't refuse the trips, we need the money."

It was then he had suggested she could have friends too. "Jeff would jump at the chance to take you out."

For the next two years I became part of her life. We were like a married couple, always together. At first Al wanted a blow-by-blow account of the time we spent together. I asked once if he still walked hand in hand with his friend along the sands.

"I don't know," she replied, "and frankly I don't care any more."

The couple were drifting further and further apart.

Then came the show when she sang in Mansfield. Someone had suggested she altered her singing style to jazz for the show. She duly obliged. It was a professionally presented show, a complete sell-out. Most of the artistes I knew well, all contacts of Millie.

For some reason I looked behind me. I saw Al sitting towards the back of the auditorium and immediately stood up and made my way towards him.

"I didn't know you were coming," I said.

"I got back earlier than I expected, and I couldn't miss this show."

I suggested that he came back with us, but he said he couldn't stay until the end because of the babysitter.

"I'll take you back then come back for Millie," I said. "I'll have to tell her, she will wonder where I have gone, then whenever you are ready we can go."

"No," he said, after a little hesitation, "she will think I am interfering. Oh, and please don't say I have been here."

"I won't say a word."

He also said something else before he went, something I thought strange and which I would remember years afterwards. He said, "You will know when she doesn't want you any more, she won't have to tell you, it'll be something you will just know."

I never gave this remark any more thought until a long while afterwards.

He brought the subject of the show up with her the following day, saying how he had been pleasantly surprised by the quality and professionalism of all the performances. It was only then that I told her he had asked me not to mention that he had been there.

It was around this time that I saw a picture of the two Italian actresses, Sophia Loren and Gina Lollobrigida, with the caption: Are these the most beautiful women in the world?

I commented, "They are not a patch on my Dusky."

Millie smiled and answered, "It's simply because you love me."

I was taken aback, it wasn't a word I had ever used, even in my mind, nor was it a word casually used, not as it is today. All I could really say was I wanted to be with her, all the time, to the exclusion of everything else.

Life continued much as before, but of course something had to happen to shatter our cosy world. I should have read the signs some weeks before. Millie told me that Al had written home to her mother, apparently telling her about our cosy relationship. 'She stops out till all hours and leaves the kids with a babysitter. All she is bothered about is the time they spend together'.

"My mother wrote to say she is disgusted. She wants nothing more to do with me."

"I'm sorry," I said, "the fault's all mine. If you want I will keep away."

'No," Millie said, defiantly.

"Well," I added, "shall I write and tell her it was his arrangement, so that he could walk along the sands with some girl who books the bus trips regularly?"

"Please don't, it will only cause more bother," she replied.

My personal feeling was that this was the little brown girl, so conveniently hidden away whilst she had her parties, and who she had been a little too ready to marry off to someone who would be forced to take her a long way off, to avoid the apartheid system that she so readily endorsed.

Her mother must have known of Millie's reluctance because of the length of time she took to finally agree to the union. Al, however, had been prepared to wait for his virginal bride.

This I gleaned from difference snippets of information I had picked up. It is always possible I had come to the wrong conclusion, but I don't think so.

A few weeks afterwards I had picked Millie up in Nottingham, as was our normal arrangement and, after the night out, returned her home. Al was waiting at the bottom of the drive; something had obviously upset him.

"You pair are making a fool of me, if you want to be together so much you had better take her. Go on, I don't want to see you again, go on, clear off."

I had no alternative but to take her back home with me, with little idea of what reception I would get from my family. I was single, living at home with my parents, and working in the family baking business. My mother had a strict idea of morality, she hadn't spoken to one of her brothers for years simply because he had got a girl pregnant. Oh, he had married her and they had a happy life. I would have thought nothing else mattered to anyone else. This turned out not to be the whole story, but it was what I believed to be true at that time. Now I was taking home a married woman. I was expecting a rough ride but I had nowhere else to go.

I had no money worth mentioning. What could I say to Millie as we made our way back along those country lanes?

None of this did I convey to the dusky beauty at my side, as we covered the miles back to my home, we didn't speak a word.

Even if I couldn't put a name to my emotions, I loved Millie more than life itself.

As we came to a halt outside the bakery I touched her hand, smiled and spoke for the first time, with a confidence I was far from feeling. "It'll be all right, I won't be long," and getting out of the van I walked down the alley and into the bakery.

Not entirely unexpectedly my father had changed and was ready for work. We had a nightshift worker who was becoming very unreliable and so dad had turned in. I would have taken over anyway, he had been advised by his doctor not to work after a series of heart attacks starting during my army service.

I got him to one side.

"I've brought a girl home, her husband has thrown her out."

He looked at me for an elaboration.

"He doesn't approve of me," I finished tamely. "We have nowhere else to go."

"Where is she going to sleep?"

"I'll do the night shift. She can use my bed."

"I'll have to tell your mother."

"I know that."

I fetched Millie and showed her to my bed.

"I'm going to have to work, we will have to sort it out in the morning, and don't worry it will be all right."

I gave her a little kiss and with little more ado left her to her own devices.

The following morning at a little after eight, before we had time to discuss what we would do, Al arrived having made the epic bus journey into Nottingham, then by tram across the city and on another bus to the village in which I lived. I would estimate a travel time of something over two hours.

I thought he must love her still. I thought of her kids and, truth be told, I was afraid I couldn't make her happy. I had even less than he had. I had weekly pocket money, which was always spent by the end of that week. The only other money I had in the whole world was the ten shillings and sixpence (fifty-two and a half pence) weekly, that had gone into the building society during the two years army national service. Everyone had to serve this in the

1950s. This money, and the interest it had accrued, amounted to about £60.

Al had asked for my thoughts on what had happened and I heard my reply. "I think you should go home, the kids are so little, they need you."

Millie was looking at me with sheer disbelief in those great brown eyes. I could hardly bear to look at her. I was behaving like a total wimp.

I couldn't imagine life without my dusky beauty, I felt absolutely wretched, and yet I couldn't see that I could do anything else. For her part Millie didn't say a word.

I drove them back to their marital home in total silence, scarcely able to steal a glance at the only woman who had ever captured my heart. Now, more than ever, I was certain that no other woman ever would.

"What are you going to do now?" Al asked.

"It rather depends. I would like to go on seeing her of course."

Neither of them spoke as they got out of the van. I wanted to ask, why now, what is different from the very first time when you suggested we went out together? I wanted to, but didn't.

I didn't go down the following Saturday night to pick her up in the place where we normally met. I felt totally and utterly bereft of any feeling, a complete wreck.

The phone call came on the Monday. It was not from Millie, it was the neighbour who usually looked after the children. She now chose to give me a piece of her mind.

"The girl is completely devastated, what are you thinking of, she doesn't deserve this." And she ranted on in much of the same vein for quite a while. When she eventually paused for breath, my father, for it was he who had picked up the phone, said, "He isn't in just now, but I will see he gets your message."

She was quiet for a while before adding, "Tell him to go to the… " she named a pub in Arnold, "I will make sure she is there."

My father was left holding the silent receiver. He put it down and the message was faithfully handed on. Dad said he thought it was Millie herself who had spoken.

"It wouldn't be," I said, "she doesn't rave. It isn't her way."

I dutifully turned up for our rendezvous at the pub. It wasn't anywhere that I had ever been before. Millie was waiting.

"Are you all right, he's being good to you isn't he?"

She seemed far away. I knew she was thinking, he doesn't want me any more.

God knows I wanted my dusky beauty more that life itself, what could I say or do?

She spoke again, "It's all right, I'm going away to London. I've got a job in a bar, it'll tide me over, and a place to stay. I have letters of introduction to some modelling agencies."

"Oh Millie, are you sure that you will be all right?"

She was only listening with half an ear, just making a statement of the facts, probably giving me the chance to say my piece. I was probably more devastated than she realized. But she was losing her kids that she adored, she was going to be the villain in most people's eyes, and I was thinking of myself, my own feelings. I was despicable.

"Who will you know, how will you manage?" I asked.

"So and so (a name I had heard mentioned before, but had never met) has arranged it for me."

"Oh," I stiffened myself, "and so you will be all right."

"If you are really interested, he is a happily married man. He has made it quite clear there isn't any chance of a romance and I don't want it. He's just going to give me help with my singing and modelling, and I always wanted to go to London at some stage. If I don't go now it'll be too late."

"I see." I had seen this altruistic attitude in other people before. The man who had spent money on getting her converted to a jazz singer for the show in Mansfield to mention just one. If Millie said there was no romantic connotations I certainly believed her.

"I thought you should know, that's all."

"What about money, at least until you get paid?"

"I would have been quite all right, but Al's taken the last lot I got from the modelling."

"How much was it?"

"Sixty pounds."

"It's all right, I'll give you the sixty pounds, that's the very least I can do."

I drove her home. It was as if we were little more that strangers.

The next day I cleared my building society account of all the money I had saved in the army, I now really had not a penny in the world, and went back the following day. When I gave it to her I had an overwhelming feeling of doing something good. It was the first gift I had ever given, not only her, but to anyone else either. She must have felt that I was buying her off, but it wasn't like that.

The world of the fifties was different, vastly different from today. You didn't take anyone out for a romantic meal, or any other meal, there was nowhere to go. People didn't have money in their pockets to buy gifts. This was the aftermath of the war, the world of the ration book, of the drabness people of today couldn't visualize. When people worked all the hours they could simply to live. When miners coming home from the pits were covered in coal muck because there weren't any baths at the pits. And they walked the streets on their way home to save the coppers needed for the bus ride home. Or drank themselves into oblivion to forget the latest roof cave-in they had just witnessed and had pulled some less fortunate soul from the coal fall. This happened more often than the public ever knew.

Oh yes, the world has changed, and not all for the better.

But it wasn't unusual to us, it was just the way it was.

I was sitting holding the hand of the woman I loved. I was worried, for her, for me. How could I have been so stupid? I really believed this girl was the only one I would ever want and I was letting her go. And at the same time I was afraid that I couldn't provide for her.

"Will you write to tell me you are all right?" I asked her.

"If that is what you want."

"I will wait for the letter," I said, and as an afterthought added, "and there isn't going to be anyone else, ever." I said it, and I meant it.

I could sense that she thought, then why are you doing this?

We actually made love, for what I believed would be the last time, on that final day. I had thrown away everything I had ever wanted, I had offered no explanation, and yet we had made love.

I didn't even look back as I left her outside her marital home, but that day my whole world came to a shuddering end.

That night, back home, I learned that the troublesome nightshift worker had eventually packed up.

"You needn't set anyone else on to do the job, I can do that, and the bread round. I won't be going out ever again," I said to my father.

He probably thought it would last a week or two, but I knew differently.

Now I began to work from ten o'clock at night, and immediately I'd finished, I went out on my deliveries. I would finish about three in the afternoon, have a meal and go straight to bed, ready to get up for my nightshift.

I wouldn't listen to music any more; the wireless, or radio as it's now called, had to be on a talk program. Every song that was broadcast was something she sang, or it had some connection with her. I wouldn't, couldn't stand it. There was one song, *I remember my September love*. No, she didn't sing that one, but we had met in September, and it had been September two years later she had left.

I was no more than a robot, a perfectly tuned working robot.

I couldn't see what else I could have done, but of course I should have been straight with her, she had a right to know.

I got my letter, brief and to the point. She had settled in, she was all right, not to worry about her. She'd be just fine.

I wrote to the address, several times. I had to know she was all right, really all right, but what business was it of mine?

All on my own I had ruined my life and I had ruined hers, it was entirely my fault.

About a month after Millie had gone, my father pointed out that I hadn't taken any wage. I told him I didn't want anything, I wasn't going to go out, I had food and a place to sleep, I wanted no more. I was too insensitive in my own cocoon to notice anything that was happening in the world around me, I was dead from the neck up.

Millie had been gone about five weeks when I had an unexpected visitor, two in fact, just as I returned from my bread rounds. It was Al and Mo, the chap who had lavished money to add another style to Millie's singing repertoire.

I looked from one face to the other, "Is she all right?" I suppose the look on my face told both of them I had no more information than they apparently had. They had obviously learned all they needed to know, and after a few pleasantries they were soon gone.

There was no bread made on Saturday night, no deliveries on Sundays. So that weekend, once I had finished work on the Saturday afternoon, I was on my way, driving the hundred and forty odd miles to the North London address. I had no idea what I would find, I had no idea what I would say, but somehow I had to know.

It was a little back street shop with adverts in the window, a forwarding address. With little or no hope of success, I went and asked about her.

"No idea mate," came back the reply. "Some of them collect their mail, others I just forward."

"But this girl?" I showed him a photo, so as to reinforce my tenuous claim.

"I don't really look at them, there are so many runaways, it's not my business. And if I did know, how long before I lost all my customers, if I gave every address away?"

I looked at him, not knowing if I wanted to choke the information out of him, or to try to bribe him. He had turned away, was serving someone else, not his problem.

The sense of anticlimax was intolerable. More people were in the shop. The hustle was pushing me towards the entrance, then I was outside. Suddenly I was so tired. It was the time I should have been asleep after my night shift. I hadn't eaten and the adrenalin was suddenly all used up.

I drove my bread van onto a piece of rubble-covered waste ground, probably the result of a German wartime bomb still waiting, like many another site, for someone or something to restore its fortunes. There I slept until the Sunday morning.

I made one more fruitless trip to the shop, when I asked if he would just tell her that Jeff came. He gave no real assurances that he would, or for that matter wouldn't. I sat in the van just down the road for a couple of hours then, thoroughly and completely drained of all emotion and feeling like an old empty shell discarded among the rest of life's garbage, I started the engine and made my way the one hundred and forty miles north to my familiar Derbyshire base. I had still got nothing to offer anyway, what could I really have said to her?

I didn't say a thing to my parents when I finally returned. A meal had been prepared for me, I ate it in total silence, and then I fell into a sound sleep on the settee. I woke as if by some signal in my brain. It was time for the nightshift, and my robotic life continued.

Several weeks later she wrote again: could I let her have the photos back she had given me, if I hadn't destroyed them, she needed them for a portfolio to get some possible modelling work.

I had about twenty or so she had given me from the last photo shoot. I sent most of them, just keeping about four, with a covering letter: how could she think I would destroy a single one, ever. I hoped she wouldn't mind me just keeping the four or so, after all it was everything I had got left now. I also told her that if she ever needed anything at all, she only had to ask. Or if she wanted me to go down I'd be there, straight away.

What a conflicting series of messages. A man who had driven her away, even given her money to go, now writing to say please let me see you, but offering nothing like the commitment she had once wanted. What she made of it I will never know.

Just after that my dad again brought up the question of money. As I said, I never had anything like a proper wage.

I repeated, "I have no need of money any more, I won't be going out ever again."

My poor kindly family must have been totally unable to know what to do. In fact there was nothing else they could have done, any intervention would have been counterproductive. They could only wait for me to 'come to my senses'. It was as if everyone was walking on eggshells.

The months went by. I saw Mo and after a few pleasantries he told me where Millie was working in London.

"She won't want to see me," I said.

"I am sure she will," he replied.

This had been the first time I had seen Mo since just after Millie had left, and I realized he must have contrived this casual meeting.

I asked dad if I could have a few weeks' pocket money, it was the first cash I'd had since my last disastrous London trip. "Of course," he replied, without asking why I wanted it.

That weekend the bread van was on another mad dash to the capital.

I pushed open the pub/club door and stood at the entrance. Millie was serving behind the bar and it was a while before I made my way towards her.

I remembered something Al had said when he had first suggested we went out together, it was so very long ago now.

"She's efficient, but somehow not really alive. She needs the stimulation of the singing, the company, the going out."

I thought I knew now, as I watched her serving behind that bar, exactly what he meant.

Now I was crossing the threshold towards her, when from the corner of my eye I saw what appeared to be a pair of bouncers purposefully moving towards me. Millie had seen me now and gave what seemed a barely perceptible nod and the two men veered off.

I was at the bar.

"I can't come straight away, I have to wait till the end of the shift," she said.

My relief was palpable. "It's all right," I said. "Everything is all right now."

Eventually it was closing time. One minute she was serving, the next she had slipped round the back of the bar and was on my side with her coat on. The same coat as she had always worn when we met in Nottingham. She was leading me purposefully towards the outside door. Once there she turned to the right and led me to a car park, no doubt expecting to find the bread van parked. But I had had to look for this place and had driven further down the road and was now parked on one of those inevitable rubble-strewn eyesores that formed the backdrop to our nation's hub.

Millie had stopped and turned to me, now she was in my arms. What happened then must be explained in the context of my state of mind. For several months my life had been on hold. I had behaved like a robot, all my actions mechanical. I could make bread, but then so could a machine if someone pressed the right buttons. I could drive, even serve customers, but I hadn't even spoken to a woman, not a recognized woman as opposed to someone who bought a loaf of bread, since I had self-destructed my whole world.

Now this dusky beauty was in my arms again, not any woman but my Dusky, the most desirable human being on the face of the planet. I felt the warmth of her body, the sensation was electric, as though I had been frozen for an eternity, and now experienced the reawakening of a sudden unexpected thaw. It was the 'eureka moment' when a daffodil bursts from the icy wastes of the frozen ground, although common sense would deem this impractical.

Of course we made love, there and then, standing where we were on the side of a London car park It was as if I heard the bells of some sweet symphony accompanying our carnal gyrations. Then what I felt was the absolute emptiness. Why was I here, I had nothing to offer? I wanted this girl more than life itself and all I could offer was poverty. Al had believed that love was enough and what had happened? The grinding poverty had driven a wedge between them, until he thought he had to ask another man to take her out.

I remember thinking, nothing's changed, I have nothing to offer. I didn't have a penny in the whole world. I wanted to give all my life to this girl she was so special and I couldn't give her a thing, only more poverty than ever. I heard again the words Al had once spoken to me, almost mocking me. Then I couldn't understand him, now I thought I could, 'you will know when she doesn't want you, she will do all the same things, but somehow you will feel rejected, you will just know'. Well it was almost like that, but it wasn't her who rejected me, it was me who rejected me. I wanted to get away from that place. I just wanted to curl up and die.

"I think I should go," I said, then turned away. I left the only woman I had ever wanted standing on a car park in the middle of London, and I would hate myself for the rest of my days.

What she made of my actions I shudder to think. I had been in a state of total euphoria all week. I had longed just to see her face, been frightened in case of rejection, then sat at that bar waiting, not knowing what would happen. It wasn't that I wanted the sexual thing, well not as a be all and end all, I wanted Millie, to be with her, to hold her, to protect her. Well, yes to love, but I hadn't even thought about it.

One minute she was there, the next we were like two animals in a frenzied orgy, and the next I was driving the one hundred and forty miles home.

Millie had wanted me to come. Mo wasn't that great a friend of mine to have delivered that sort of message unless Millie had intended that he should. I thought about it all the following week. What if I had read all the signs wrong? I thought about that place where she worked. Things weren't going that well. I thought of the worn coat, a relic from her days growing up in the sunshine of her South African youth. I thought of the girl I loved, pulling pints in that bar. Of Al saying, "Oh yes, she's efficient in everything she does, but she needs the stimulation, the excitement of the singing, the acclamation, then she is alive, she positively glows."

I decided to do the silliest thing I'd ever done in my life,

I'd go to London again. If I got past the heavies, if she was there, if I got the chance to speak to her, if she would even speak to me, I'd do the thing I should have done at the start.

I'd tell her my whole story. I'd also tell her I loved her more than life itself, that I wanted to live with her, I wanted to marry her, I wanted her anyway I could have her. I would say there needn't be any more sex, not until she needed it, longed, as I longed for the merest touch, that told us both that life had begun again. Then the choice would be hers alone. I would make her understand every action I had taken and why.

Once more the bread van was on its way to that North London pub.

Chapter 2

My story, or perhaps I should begin with my dad's story, because only then would she understand.

My father had been called up into the Great War of 1914-1918, and had found himself in the trenches of France at a time when few actually came back to tell the tales of the horror of the Somme, or Passchendaele. He was just sixteen. His own father had written letters about this boy who should never have been there, then suddenly he had been sent back, already suffering with pneumonia, or trench fever as it was described then. The same trench fever that killed more of our lads than the Germans ever did.

The War Department announced that it had been a case of mistaken identity. Someone of the same name had been identified and was drafted in to take his place in the killing fields.

At eighteen, now fully recovered, he was sent back to rejoin the ranks of the living dead.

Dad survived, unlike many of his colleagues, and was repatriated. He returned home to the land Lloyd George had said would be fit for heroes to live in.

Nothing had altered.

Granddad was a farmer and dad had perhaps expected to resume working on the family farm. But other younger siblings had grown up and were fulfilling those duties. Granddad had a solution however. He was also something of a wheeler-dealer. On the edge of the farm was a row of properties, there were shops, work premises etc. He had bought them as a job lot and among them was a disused bakery. The place was dilapidated and there were holes in the roof of both the bakery and the adjoining living quarters.

"You can be a baker," he announced. "You will have somewhere to sleep as well."

"I don't know the first thing about the job," dad said.

"No problem, go out and get a job in some bakery for a month or two, then you can get going."

Dad looked around the place, with its leaky roof and things just pushed aside so they didn't get too wet and unusable. It wasn't exactly a heaven-sent opportunity, but thousands who returned from the Great War would have even less. And if you didn't do anything you didn't eat, this was just the way it was for everybody. The men who had risked life and limb, cannon-fodder in the national hour of need, were just so many more competing for whatever work was in the market place.

Dad got his job, learned his new trade, and some six months later was his own man, to sink or swim by his new-found abilities. At the time, almost every other housewife made a few loaves for herself and her neighbours, supplementing her husband's often limited financial remunerations from whatever work she could find.

Dad began work, mixing and kneading dough by hand at four o'clock each day. Then tinning the individual portions and trying to keep them something like warm in that leaky, draughty building (the part that had been the stables) so that they would rise enough to bake for a professional finish. Then he had to deliver the bread in his van (at a time when most of the others had just a horse and dray) and sell sufficient to earn enough to survive in the harsh economic climate. Each day, when he returned, he would climb up onto the roof to do what repairs he could, to try to insulate the place against the elements. Hopefully before the onset of a winter's cold that could render all attempts to make bread no more than a distant memory.

There still was no electricity on line throughout the district. So dad bought his own generator, rigged up his mixer, and then had the mechanical means to mix his bread doughs. He was improving all the time.

This stuttering start to his career would again be put in jeopardy some six years into his adventure when, in 1926, the mining bosses, no doubt with their own pressures, decided to reduce the wages of the men who hewed the valued mineral, with little more than a pick and shovel, from the unending tunnels in the bowels of the earth.

The miners laid down their tools, with the rallying cry, 'Not an hour on the day, not a penny off the pay'. The collieries ground to a halt and the womenfolk hadn't even the few coppers needed to buy the basic foodstuffs to prevent starvation.

So much for the grandiose oratory, and the dreams of our political masters to carve themselves a reflected place in the nation's psyche.

If dad baked bread no one could buy it, if he didn't he was finished anyway. The solution was to bake some and hope that the recipients, even if they didn't pay, would at least retain some sort of loyalty. The chances that they would ever get enough to pay any back money just flew in the face of convention.

The fledgling trade unions brought out the rest of industry in a show of solidarity, the nation shuddering to a halt in the great strike of 1926. But with the best will in the world the support of other trades could only be transitory, they also had mouths to feed. There were enough stocks of coal above ground to feed the demands of industry for some time. So if the big colliery bosses had enough wealth, they just left these shores and took extended holidays in the warmth of some foreign sun.

Any 'blacklegs' who tried to defy the picket lines and alleviate the suffering of their families, endured some frightful beatings, deaths were not unheard off.

It was well into 1927 before the strike was broken and miners again doffed their caps to their 'betters', took their reduced wages, and crawled back into the dangerous underground labyrinths.

Those workers' leaders, who only wanted to preserve the living standards, were now singled out by the bosses and most never worked again.

My dad weathered the crisis and by 1930 he had a bride. She insisted that the house was weatherproof before she took the plunge into matrimony. However, the place must have been habitable by the middle of June, and the wedding took place at the new church, built by a local miner who had made his fortune as a union man, after emigrating to America.

Things took another unexpected turn the following year. My grandfather had died in 1929, but there had been no indication of what would be revealed in his will. Among his extensive holdings, as well as the farm and dad's bakery, he had a share in another farm, some houses, a part of another bakery, and numerous other properties.

Dad had always paid rent, but understood the family home and bakery would always be his. He was in for another nasty surprise. It seemed that when my grandmother had died some years earlier she had said, "They can all work to earn a living." The youngest of her nine surviving kids, however, was a weakling and grandfather must look after him.

He took it as gospel and the entire estate now passed to my uncle, who lavished it on Rolls Royce cars and a female entourage. Mother was less than pleased, but apparently dad simply said, "It's his money to dispose of as he wishes."

Uncle Tom casually remarked one day, "I've no use for this bakery, I'm putting it on the market."

"This is my home, you know, not just my work," dad had replied. He had been paying his rent and probably expected to be allowed to carry on as he always had.

As if anticipating a similar reply, Tom announced the valuation figure which he had obtained.

"You know I don't have that sort of money," dad replied.

"I didn't think you had, that's why it is going on the market, you can bid with anyone else. Who knows, you might even get it cheaper."

Dad looked at his kid brother who was throwing money around with no thought for the future.

"All right, I'll see what I can borrow."

"I thought you might," Tom replied.

Dad managed to obtain a mortgage and began buying the property he had always been told was his own.

Still the struggles continued.

I came into the world in 1932 and my sister some seven years later.

Dad was forty at the outbreak of the Second World War. Just old enough to escape another period in the armed forces, but he still had to do his Dad's Army bit. Everyone had a spell of 'territorial' and fire-fighting training, and everyone in turn had to walk the streets during the hours of darkness to ensure no chinks of light escaped to reveal any evidence of human presence to enemy bombers. This was called the 'black-out'.

They also built artificial decoys, miles from strategically important spots, which did allow light to escape, supposedly attracting the bombs. The difficulty was the Germans weren't that accurate anyway and the ruins in all the major conurbations showed these targets were too extensive to miss.

Everything was supposed to ensure readiness for an invasion many thought wasn't far away.

Doctors, hospitals, businesses and limited essential workers had some petrol, but the general public, if they were lucky enough to own a car, simply 'moth-balled' their vehicles in readiness for the end of hostilities. Many an old car would show up years later simply buried in the hay of an agricultural barn, often with very low mileage registered on the clock.

As a business we had petrol for our work needs, but this was severely restricted for any private use.

Father had learned enough German during the First World War to understand the language broadcasts and was able to form a balanced view of how the conflict was progressing. He could often be seen with the crackly old wireless, listening to reports in a variety of different languages.

Once I said, "I didn't know you understood that."

He replied, "You pick it up a little here and there."

He seemed to be able to, but it was a knack I have never mastered.

In our neck of the woods, those of us too young or too old to be drafted weren't actually called-up to fight and didn't suffer too much, though everyone had a brother or a father who had gone.

Women also were sent to serve, as a back-up, either in the army, navy, or air force. They also worked on the land, or in the munitions factories, usually drafted far away from their friends and families, in distant parts of the country.

Another group displaced from their environments were the 'Bevin boys', sent to the coalfields to dig the precious mineral from the earth. Why were they sent there instead of the front-line? Only the authorities seemed aware of what lottery of perverse thinking designated their action. As a very young boy I had spoken to one of these miners who had said he had a pilot's license and had been a flier since a very early age. All he had ever wanted was to fight in the air force.

We grew up in this rarefied world of the very young and the very old. We all knew kids whose fathers or big brothers had gone to war, leaving behind families who waited for the dreaded postman's knock and the abrupt telegram which told them their loved ones were killed in action.

Another set of strangers catapulted into our midst were the evacuees, those kids uprooted from their own families in the bombing areas. They were placed with families who had the capacity to house them. Some fitted in, some didn't, depending both on their temperaments and those of the families who housed them.

Food was rationed, cakes non-existent. Sugar was a rarity and one shilling and twopence (about 6p) worth of meat was the ration. Bread was now made with a greyish-coloured flour and also on ration. However, in country districts like ours most of the vegetables were home grown. We were told by Government experts that our diet was 'the best in human history' and we would live far longer than any previous generations. I don't know how they expected to convince those who endured the nightly bombings in all the main cities. Even to those of us who escaped the destruction, this was something the aged speakers couldn't ever expect to know if their words were vindicated. I suppose that rather depended on future leaders not having any dreams of winning wars.

We had our gas-masks, old Hitler was going to gas the lot of us. We had all been taught how to put them on, even from the smallest of kids, and had practice sessions at school.

Air raid shelters had been dug everywhere. As kids at school we had drill in getting inside the 'Anderson shelter', which was in the school grounds, as soon as possible after the sirens sounded. But for us kids it was something of a game, nothing seemed serious.

There was the Dig for Victory campaign. Every spare bit of land was cultivated to grow food. Most households had chickens, or pigs in sheds, some very close to the door. All scraps of leftover food were fed to the livestock. No one grew flowers, it had to be something to help to feed the family. Everyone who was capable tried to get an allotment. This was a piece of ground to grow their vegetables. These were worked again by old men, or in some cases old women. In this way most families, especially in the rural places, managed well enough.

This was our war.

There was no 'tele' to relay the horrors of the conflict, to show the way our cities had been flattened, or the coffins that held the mangled bodies of our servicemen. It was too late ask them to give their views.

We heard the defiant utterances of Winston Churchill, which always seemed to give everyone a lift. We had the feeling that everything would be all right in the end.

The war ended in 1945. It was as abrupt as that. It was suddenly all over. But it was a long time before the servicemen returned to compete in the work market.

I left school in 1946, still a month short of my fourteenth birthday, and started work, firstly as a van lad at the bakery.

We had a motley crew of bakers. If we needed a baker, right from the war period, we had to apply at the dole office. They would then allocate a worker, if someone happened to be available.

Our nightshift consisted of a Pole, a Ukrainian chap who claimed to be related to the Russian Romanovs, and a repatriated soldier who had lost a leg. He brought his wife to work while he sat supervising. He called her 'woman', screamed at her, and generally treated her like dirt. Also we had a man who had only one eye. He had a pot one, which he would take out and polish. I was horrified the first time I saw this and never could really come to terms with it.

Rather surprisingly the whole thing seemed to work well, the point being they all wanted to work. And they worked long hours, as was the custom of the time. The bread was always got out in the morning. There was still no confectionery made but I remember the odd occasions when we had enough sugar to bake some queen cakes. There were queues right down the road.

There were ten bakeries in the village and the neighbouring town of Alfreton at the end of the war. By 1949, when dad bought up the only other one left, there was only us still delivering our produce.

Dad had bought new machinery and we were going along quite nicely. This was the period when the big multi-national bakers were taking all before them with their mass-produced goods, and seemingly unlimited financial backing. Then dad had an offer from one of them to take over the place, it seemed too good to resist. Dad could retire and be comfortably off. At fifty he would never need to work again.

Talks had reached a final stage, the money was on the table. It was then I said I had always expected the chance to run the business. Dad immediately cancelled negotiations. However, I was now seventeen and the following year I was called up for the mandatory two years national service. I had no option but to go. I wasn't a particularly good soldier, doing just enough to keep out of trouble, but I served my time, until I could get out and resume my chosen profession. But things didn't quite work out the way I had expected.

I hadn't been away long when dad had the first of his heart attacks. They would happen once or sometimes twice yearly for the next sixteen years. He followed all the medical advice, but knowledge wasn't so good then and nothing seemed to work.

Without a strong hand to guide the staff there were the inevitable clashes of personality. Deliveries became less certain, production was haphazard, customers were lost, wastage increased, cases of pilfering became rampant, profits soon vanished.

We still had the five vans out every day, but every one was barely covering costs. I returned to a vastly different world.

Even when most of the problems were ironed out, still there was the problem of customer confidence. That was going to take a little more than soothing words, especially with the cheap flood of bread, delivered on a sale-or-return basis by the multi-nationals to all our clients.

Times were going to be hard for the foreseeable future. The whole point being, I could not try something else because dad was ill. He could have been retired two years before and it would have been a comfortable retirement, with no financial worries. Just maybe, and who ever knows about these things, he might never have had his heart attacks. Instead, because I wanted to run the place he had tried to give me a chance. Now, with no money to speak of, we were both trapped into trying to make the best of things. I didn't know if I could make things work in the long run, and I felt that I dare not bring the woman I loved more than life itself into a situation where I might condemn her to spend years in poverty. I knew my father would have been the last person to keep me to my side of the bargain, but I just couldn't walk away. Well I'd said I wanted the bakery.

Chapter 3

The van was on its way and I was in all sorts of turmoil, considering what I was going to say. It seemed a hopeless task, but at least it would be Millie's decision. I saw a sign indicating I had crossed the county boundary and I was in Northamptonshire. This was odd because the sign was old and partially covered in the undergrowth. There shouldn't have been any pre-war indication of place names. They had all been taken up during the conflict so that any invading force wouldn't know where they were. That was the theory anyway.

Everything was playing on my mind

A blood-red car overtook me, a little too fast, a little too close to a bend. The blonde girl who was driving even waved as she sped away into the night. She mustn't do that too often. There wasn't that many vehicles travelling along the roads, but still you could have accidents. Tiny things were irritating me that normally I wouldn't even notice.

Further down that road I saw some smoke rising over a hedge and upon rounding a bend I saw the red car had indeed been involved in a smash and had turned over. Pulling up, I ran towards the accident. A man was sitting in a black car which was displaying a big dent just where he was sitting. He was staring straight ahead and a little blood had trickled onto his black moustache. He appeared like a waxwork copy of Oliver Hardy, from the Laurel and Hardy duo of comedians. He certainly didn't seem real and I didn't give him much more than a glance as I ran by.

It was the red car standing partly on its side and roof, on a grassy bank, from which the smoke was now coming. I grabbed hold of the door handle. It seemed to be jammed so I put a foot on the side of the car, levered myself and pulled again with the strength of a maniac. Luckily this time it flew open and I fell onto the bank and rolled slightly. Then, jumping up I reached through the now open door and pulled at the girl. Her foot was stuck, probably under the pedals. The smoke made me gasp and I drew back and got a lungful of the fresh air. Maybe memory was playing a trick, but it seemed to me there was an awful lot of smoke. I was getting frantic, she had to get out of that car. I wrapped my arms round the leg which was jammed, then another huge pull and I was on the bank, the girl on top of me in a somewhat ungainly heap.

Throughout all this time her hair had been hanging across the front of her face. It was even now as I pulled myself from under her, rolled away, then all in the same movement dragged her away from her car with about as much consideration as I would have given a bag of potatoes.

Even if I had seen the girl again, it's doubtful if I could have recognized her, I never saw her face.

The car was still smoking and suddenly there were people coming from all directions. Someone had a fire extinguisher (an unusual contraption that I had never seen before) which he now sprayed onto the car engine. There was a great cloud of steam, black smoke, and general dirt which pothered into the air and people jumped away.

Now it seemed as if I wasn't part of the proceedings, like a bystander on the periphery of the events. Nothing seemed real, all these people scurrying about. There was a chatter of voices, I was in a haze, which nothing penetrated. Then, something seemed to be shaking my arm and I gathered my wits. It was a woman thumping her little fists into my shoulder. She was saying something now, my scattered wits picked up some words.

"You could have killed her, what were you doing?"

I was slowly getting some sense of reality.

"It's nothing to do with me." I wasn't feeling like taking the blame, whatever she thought I was guilty of. I grabbed the wrists, stopping her pounding me. Now I could hear the siren sound of an approaching ambulance. The woman's hysteria had subsided into a gentle sobbing.

A man's voice said, "You will have to go to the hospital, they'll check you for the shock." He turned and walked away.

I had no intention of going to any hospital. I backed away then turned and, without even a glance at 'Oliver', made my way back to the van. No one seemed even interested in either me or the black car. I started the engine, turned left up a street and the van moved off into the night.

I would never know the outcome of that night, how either of the two principals in the drama fared. Were they walking around and laughing about it a week or two later, or did neither of them ever take another breath?

I felt cold when I woke, even though the sun was high overhead. The van was badly parked, partly in and out of the garage at the bakery. I must have fallen asleep from long working hours, I had obviously slept there all night. I'd been going to see Millie to try to sort things out, but I'd had the strangest dream. Once more I had let down the dusky beauty that I loved.

Wearily I walked across the road. My family didn't seem to be around. The door was open and I went in, glancing at myself in the mirror. It was a shock. My face was black like a chimney sweep's. Automatically I reached to touch my face and saw that my right hand was covered with blood and my thumb was sticking out at some odd angle. I rushed to the bathroom to examine myself closer.

The blood seemed to have come from a cut across the back of my wrist. It looked big then, today I would be hard-pressed to find the scar. The hair on the front of my head seemed to have been singed, but how can you burn anything without fire? My left ear was double its normal size. It was as if I had walked into a bus. I couldn't explain just how or when I got any of my battle scars.

One thing was certain, this had been no dream, but how I had driven myself home I shall never know, even to this day. I have no idea either, nor would I ever know, what happened either to 'Oliver' or the blonde girl.

I cleaned myself up as best I could, slipped downstairs, and making sure I wasn't seen, drove to the local cottage hospital. A doctor who examined me announced that my thumb was dislocated, seemed to pull it, I let out a scream, but it had done the job. It now looked normal, though the hand certainly seemed strangely twisted. It was terribly weak for some while afterwards. I asked about the ear and, with little more than a glance, he got a long needle and stuck it right through the middle and out the other side. A nurse who had been standing beside him now cleaned it up, stuck a plaster on it, and announced it would be OK.

The doctor, without even a goodbye, had already left to practise his own brand of rough medicine elsewhere. This man apparently enjoyed his work.

The nurse said, "You really should be in bed, you look as if you need some rest."

I didn't tell them I was driving, or they would probably have tried to stop me. The van was waiting and I got behind the wheel and drove home. I again dodged my parents, slipped upstairs, threw off my clothes and took the nurse at her word.

The next thing I remembered was lying in my bed with another doctor standing looking at me. It seemed my family had sent for him and both mother and dad were standing there.

"He's waking," mother said.

It seemed a daft thing to say. Of course I was waking up.

The doctor put his stethoscope to my chest.

"What's happening"? I asked. "It's time I got to work."

Dad spoke, "It's all right, I've sorted it out."

The doctor said, "You will be all right with a little rest," and he handed me a cup with some vile-tasting liquid. I drank it to humour him, I just wanted him to go away.

When I eventually woke again my body was wet with sweat. I was hungry as well. Going to the bathroom I filled the sink with hot water. I was starting to wash my face when I saw that my ear looked even larger and more grotesque than previously.

What would my family say? I thought. Somehow I never connected they must have seen it. I dried myself and slipped back into bed.

It was dad who came up. "I thought I heard you. Do you want something bringing up, or will you be getting up?" he asked.

I got up. I couldn't hide away for ever.

To their eternal credit neither of my parents even mentioned my disfigurement, but I'm sure they thought it must be something to do with Millie. A lot of other people did though. It was mainly to the effect, 'What does the other fellow look like?'

Another trip to the doctor and another needle reduced the ear to normal, but once more it was the same the following day. After a third visit, and a trip to hospital in which they injected something into it, today, although it doesn't look quite right, at least it is presentable.

It would be some time afterwards before I found out I'd spent three days in some sort of delirium and that the doctor had attended every day. (I shudder to think of what anyone made of anything I might have said.)

I began to work again.

Several weeks afterwards I'd been tinkering with one of the machines. It was Sunday morning, the only time I had to do any maintenance. Satisfied now that it was at least better, I washed my hands and went in for my dinner.

My parents were already seated and also at the table was a girl I hadn't seen since my tennis-playing days, which was before my national service, maybe five years before. She often used to come and watch while I was playing. I knew all about her background, everyone did locally. She was an only daughter, the heiress to a multi-millionaire family, probably the richest in the area.

Why was she here? She wasn't anything to do with me.

I picked at the food on my plate, decided I wasn't hungry any more, pushed it away, got up and walked out.

Later dad asked me what was wrong. "She seems a nice girl," he added.

"She is a nice girl," I agreed. He looked at me totally unable to comprehend my actions. "Oh, I haven't a penny to my name, I couldn't even afford to buy the clothes she wears." It was true, but not the real reason. I walked away, that should have been enough to satisfy him.

What I had said obviously got relayed to her family. I knew her mother of course. Well, I knew her by sight, I'd never spoken to her. A few days later I saw her on the street and as I was walking by she stopped me.

"Whoever has my daughter won't need to find the money for her clothes. In fact, any money she wants, for any reason, she can have."

I didn't know what to say. She could buy anything she wanted, and obviously for her only daughter, nothing was too much. I should have said, "I'm sorry, but I'm not for sale," but I didn't. I don't think I even answered, I just walked away.

Back at home I cornered my father. "Don't you even begin to understand, not even now?"

"She is a very beautiful woman." He was talking about Millie.

I could feel the 'but' coming, I didn't let him carry on.

"Millie's more than just a beautiful woman, she is an angel. I should rot in hell for what I did to her. I thought surely you must realize by now, I don't want any other woman, ever."

This was the first time I had ever heard my dad say any woman was beautiful, and I would never hear him say it about any other woman.

I decided to tell the heiress the reason for my ignorance. It certainly must have seemed like that. I couldn't say to her mother, "I'm sorry, but your virginal daughter isn't good enough, no other woman will ever be good enough. You see I'm hopelessly in love with someone else, only she happens to be the wife of another man and the mother of his two children. And worse than that, I let her down and she's gone away, and I probably won't ever see her again."

I would tell the daughter, perhaps not in those words, but I would make her realize the way I felt, and that I wouldn't change my mind. That day must have been a terrible embarrassment to her, I would have spared her if I had known. When I got the opportunity I would try to explain, that much I certainly owed her.

I didn't tell her because I never saw her again, it was as if she had vanished off the map.

Chapter 4

I carried on with my new lifestyle. I never went out, I did my job. Looking back, it must have been terrible for my kindly family. They must have been 'walking on eggshells'.

I'd say now, were it not too late, "I'm so very sorry, for the way I shut you both out."

They had this strange son, who couldn't bear to hear any popular songs, never went out, and I would now find out, had developed a phobia about blonde-haired women. If I saw a blonde coming towards me I'd see she had no face, just blonde hair where a face should have been. I would break out in a cold sweat and turn away. Sometimes I even imagined she was lying on the grass and I could smell the smoke again. I would turn and walk away, hoping no one had seen my sheer panic.

A few weeks afterwards I saw my building society book lying on the top of the desk. I picked it up, I might as well throw it away. Casually I opened it. My father must have looked inside, after all, I'd made such a show of saying I hadn't anything in the world, he would have found out it was the truth. Now it was me that was in for a surprise. I wouldn't take any money so, from the day the heiress came to dinner, he had increased my pocket money to £10 and saved it in the building society every week. My first reaction was to draw it out and give it him back. But it wasn't his fault that I'd ruined my life, and I had upset him enough, it could stay.

Then something else happened. I'd taken my van to the garage for some repairs. I was speaking to one of the mechanics who told me about this chap who wanted to buy a car that they had for sale.

"As a bankrupt he can't get any credit and he needs this old banger to get to his work. Don't suppose you would like to help? He'll pay the normal rate of interest."

I was about to walk away when he added, "It's only fifty quid."

I stopped. This was the same amount that was standing in my building society account.

"Why don't you do it then?" I asked him.

"I can't afford to lend anyone fifty pounds."

"How much is the interest did you say?"

"Twenty percent. Or, if you like, 10% over six months." He saw me wavering and added, "I've got a proper form, all straight and legal." He produced a pile of forms from the desk. "He'll get in all sorts of bother just for taking out another loan if anybody found out, so it's a certainty that he'll pay up."

He was as good as gold paying every payment on time, and I had made ten pounds in just six months(that was almost a weekly wage). He recommended another customer for me so I registered the company and the Midland Finance Company was born.

I now had ten pounds a week I could invest, plus the repayments as they came in.

The way a finance company works, and why it works so well, is that for every payment I received it was immediately reinvested. So, before the amount is repaid, say over a one year period, there are already eleven other people repaying the original amount. I found that I could double every pound I had invested every twelve and a half months.

The next thing that happened was a tax demand so I asked to see the tax inspector. This had been against the insistent advice of the bakery's accountant. When I was shown into the official's office, I don't know just what he, or I expected, but I was confident of my argument.

"I have no money," I told him. "Every penny I earn goes straight to the finance company and its total assets are still less than two hundred pounds."

"Why do you want to lend money, if you have none?" he enquired, totally perplexed.

"That's the reason, if I don't try something then I will never have any money."

"Does it pay?" he asked.

"Of course, but when I started I had fifty pounds to my name, I've still got nothing, but the company has got money owing to it. Eventually there will be money, but now it's all on paper."

"When do you expect to have some money to pay taxes?"

"Well, I suppose eventually I will have to pay something, but by then I will have something for myself as well."

I'm not sure what he made of my arguments, but at least he agreed to do nothing. "We will have to review this at some time in the future," were his parting words.

I shook his hand, thanked him for his time, and walked outside.

"And did he accept that?" the accountant asked later.

"Of course. I told him the truth and of course he accepted it. What else could he have done?"

"You have got the nerve of the devil, I wouldn't have tried that."

"You should always go for the honest truth," I told him, but he looked dubious.

It was only a matter of weeks later, when I had two separate people asking me if they could invest in the finance company. So I got two thousand pounds off each of them and I paid them a straight 10% per annum. I'm sure they would have had second thoughts if they had known they had lent to a company whose total assets were less than two hundred pounds.

Now I was paying 10% per year, and I still kept their money. I could almost double it that time, and I could still use that money. Even so, I eventually found that I had more customers than I could cope with.

Later on I went to the bank asking for an ongoing loan, explaining the purpose I needed it for. He was most sympathetic, but explained the bank's policy was not to lend to someone who was re-lending it. And he added, "It won't be any good going to another bank." I would find out it was common banking policy.

Not to worry, I was doing very nicely anyway. As I got up to leave, he said, "I could lend you some money for property repairs."

"I've no property to repair."

He smiled. "And how am I supposed to know that?"

I now had an overdraft of three thousand pounds.

I worked in a professional way. Every customer was properly checked out at a finance agency. I had my letters which I sent to late payers, and another letter written in a more demanding way if that didn't bear fruit. I was getting more than 99% of my money. And if anyone suddenly 'did a runner' I had a detective who could find them.

I still worked all night and half the day, the only concession was that I now had a van lad who certainly made things a little easier. Later on I taught him to drive, so he was the driver, and sometimes I was even asleep as he did the driving, I don't suppose that was strictly legal, a learner driver with a sleeping instructor, but it certainly happened.

I still had no social life at all, nor did I want one. I still wouldn't listen to the radio playing songs. I must have seemed an 'odd-ball'.

This carried on until the spring of 1960. It was three and a half years since Millie went away. It was five and a half years since I first walked into that lido clubroom and totally altered my life. It wasn't that I had Millie on my mind now. I simply wasn't allowing myself to think about the woman I loved, at all. In fact I wasn't even letting myself think.

The unlikely catalyst to alter my life again, was an old gossipy woman, who knew everybody's business, and what she didn't know she made up. I've never liked these sort of people, and I'm still not too keen.

I'd just finished my rounds. For once there was no finance business to sort out so I'd have my dinner and go to bed. It was then that I overheard this old Nosey Parker talking to one of our shop assistants. The conversation went something like this.

"Doesn't he even have a girlfriend?"

"I don't know, I've never seen him with one."

"Do you think he's one of them 'funny-people'?"

I'd heard enough. I walked in. "Is there something you want to ask me?"

She was flustered. "I was only making conversation." She gathered her things and made for the door.

"You had better make sure of your facts before you open your mouth again".

The door closed, and she was gone.

"People like her should be locked up in a lunatic asylum."

The young girl was looking at me a bit oddly.

I retreated into the house. I'd never considered what anyone might have thought of me, now I was bothered. Those with 'odd' tendencies could be, and often were, locked up in the 1950s. I could certainly due without gossipy old women shouting their mouths off.

For about the first time since I began my marathon work regime I could not sleep.

I knew what I had to do. That Saturday after a few hours sleep, I decided to go out for the first time in three and a half years. Mansfield was the obvious choice. It would be unlikely that any of my old friends were still around the place now. The idea was simply to be seen with some girls. Nothing would happen, but the 'heat' would be off. I couldn't go to dances any more, I couldn't bear to hold a girl in my arms.

Oh, so much for the best laid plans, of mice and men.

The girl, who had shoulder-length black hair (I still had this phobia about blondes, though it wasn't quite so bad now), was standing at the bar talking to Alan. He was a mate of mine from a long time ago. He looked up when he saw me. "Hi, have you made an honest woman of that South African girl yet?"

"I wish I could. I managed to mess it all up, she's gone now."

"Where've you been then?"

"Working all the hours God sends, trying to forget what an idiot I am."

"Still got it bad then?"

"Have a drink, and one for the lady friend."

It was a subject I didn't want to discuss. They both accepted the drink.

He introduced her, though for the life of me I can't remember her name now. Alan had wandered off and I would monopolize her attention for the rest of the night. Then it was time to go and I looked for Alan. "We seem to have lost your boyfriend," I said.

"He isn't my boyfriend, just someone I talk to sometimes."

She didn't seem to be with anyone else.

I asked her, "How are you getting home?"

"By bus," came back the reply.

I found out where she lived.

"I'll take you back if you like."

So now she was in the bread van. We pulled up just before we reached the village where she lived. She was in my arms. In the half-light, and with the long black hair, I held her body close to mine. It had been so long ago. Of course we made love, and I was violently sick, not once, but several times. I couldn't ever remember any occasion when I had been sick before.

I kept repeating, "I'm sorry, I'm very sorry, I didn't mean that to happen."

She replied, "It was what we both wanted to happen."

It wasn't what I wanted to happen. I took her to her home and drove away.

It was a long time before I went to sleep that night. I mulled over the events of the night in my mind. Was I so shallow that the first girl with long black hair could make me forget the woman I loved? The sun was already rising before I fell into a restless sleep.

Millie could have been divorced and remarried by now, for all I knew. Three and a half years is a long time.

On the Monday as I came back from the rounds my father greeted me. He mentioned the girl's name. "She phoned, seemed very concerned about you, said the beer had been off and you hadn't been very well."

"I suppose that could have been one interpretation."

I wanted to walk away.

"She seemed a very nice girl."

My father obviously saw some hope that I was getting over what must have been a nightmare period for both my parents.

During the week I thought about what had happened. I didn't see anyone else being sick that night, so the beer was one theory that could be discounted. I wondered if every girl I touched would have the same effect. After all, I had sworn there wouldn't be another girl and that I would wait for ever for a miracle that I knew couldn't ever happen.

I suppose there was a more likely scenario, and one that I never considered. It wasn't only Millie that I hadn't seen for three and a half years, I had never touched a drop of alcohol in the whole of that time.

Once more I went to Mansfield on the Saturday, I would put it to the test. I don't think I would have recognized the girl from the previous week. I don't think I saw her but another girl was in my arms, her name was Margaret. This time the events of the night proved similar, but I wasn't sick. She was young, only about seventeen to my twenty-eight, as one of her neighbours was quick to point out to me when I pulled up outside her home.

This girl lasted longer, maybe a couple of months, but I suddenly told her I couldn't see her again.

"Why, what have I done? I'll change, I'll be whatever sort of girl you want me to be. Are you ashamed of me?"

"No one could ever be ashamed of you, and whatever you do, don't change anything, not for me, or for anyone else."

"Then why?" she asked

"It's not you, it's me. I'm just no good."

"Everybody said you would chuck me."

"Tell anyone who says that, you have chucked me."

"They wont believe that."

"They will, if I tell them as well." I kissed her goodbye and drove away.

I didn't go to Mansfield the next weekend.

During the following week she arrived at the bakery. Once more someone had made a marathon bus journey, catching three buses which probably didn't have a very good connection between them. I came in from my rounds and she was sitting at the table, my family had done their best to make her welcome.

"Why have you come?" I asked, trying not to be unkindly.

"I had to try again, I love you."

"Oh please, don't."

"Your family aren't ashamed of me."

"Don't do that again. I'm not ashamed of you, I think you are a lovely girl, but I cannot see you again." Her eyes were starting to fill with tears and I passed her a hanky. "Come on I'll take you home."

It wouldn't help my sleeping arrangements but I'd no option.

I didn't go into Mansfield on the following Saturday either, so it was several weeks afterwards that I next saw her.

A friend of hers came over to me and said, "I hear Margaret's chucked you."

"Yes, she thinks I'm a little too old for her."

"Well I'm available, and I don't think you're too old."

Margaret, who was sitting nearby, overheard this and instantly burst into tears.

I didn't go to Mansfield for a long time afterwards.

Still, I soon found another girl to share my Saturday nights. The pattern was very similar. After about six or seven weeks, I again broke it off. There was perhaps half a dozen girls altogether who shared my Saturdays during 1960, all probably, if truth were known, deserved someone far better than I could ever have been. What triggered the end of our relationships I would have been hard pressed to explain. But in at least one of these, there had been tears.

Half a dozen girls all with black, or at least dark, hair who gave all a woman can give, body and soul. It was never enough.

I was beginning to despise myself, how could I be so callous? I was starting to think there was something fundamentally wrong with me. I was still waiting for the one girl who I had loved.

I suddenly noticed something else. Every one of those girls had the same initials as Millie. Either MH, which was her own name, or MM her stage name. It seemed impossible, but it was true. The gods of chance seemed to be playing a strange game with me.

Well, it was then that I made a conscious decision. If it was the sex thing that caused this overflowing of emotions, then I would do without it.

My next 'Saturday-night-friend' was a girl who collected some goods quite regularly. She asked me if I would go to a party a member of her family was having. It was a birthday bash, she told me.

There was no more than the most tentative peck on the cheek exchanged between us during the whole night. And nothing more would happen to stir any latent emotions than had on that first encounter. It hadn't happened then, and I hadn't the slightest feeling that it ever would.

From that day she always contrived to find some reason why we should meet, or I should be in a place where she was. Then, a while afterwards, one of her girl friends said, "No woman will forgive you for not trying it on."

I can't remember how I replied, but the plain truth was I hadn't the slightest interest in 'trying it on'. I carried on going to see her. For one thing, she kept buying heaps of bread and buns.

Then one day her mother announced they would be going away for the weekend. "It will be all right if you want to stay here on the Saturday night."

I didn't think mothers suggested things like that, but I didn't stop there.

One day her friend said, "I know you are waiting until you get engaged, but you don't have to."

"You seem very well informed about what we do."

"Girls talk you know."

"I see."

I didn't want this conversation.

Then it was her twenty-first birthday party. Of course I was there, the place was full of her friends, her family, and all sorts of people. I had arrived a little late and walked up to the bar. There was entertainment, then the music stopped. The DJ needed to make an announcement and he had the microphone in his hand.

"This isn't just a twenty-first birthday party." I looked up mildly interested, then the spotlight swung round and I was in the full glare of the beam. "It's also an announcement of the engagement to Jeff."

The glass which was in my hand I now put down and made my way across the back of the room, the light still following me. But instead of turning towards the stage I went straight on, through the door and outside. I stood there for a minute, breathing in the night air. No one had followed me outside. I walked across to the waiting bread van, the engine roared into life, I turned the steering wheel and drove into the road. I didn't go far, turning into the driveway of the next pub. I'd have a quiet drink before going home.

A voice behind me said, "I didn't think you would do that." Her brother had obviously followed me.

"Did you know she was going to do that?" I asked.

"She should have told you."

"Well she didn't."

"She is very upset, you could talk about it."

"I think it's better to let things stay as they are now, it would only give her the wrong impression."

He looked as if he was going to say something else, decided against it, turned away and walked out of the place.

Looking back, I don't see what else I could have done. I heard some time later on that she had a mental breakdown. If I in any way contributed, then I would have another regret to carry to my grave.

It seemed that it wasn't just the sex I had to steer clear of. I decided there wouldn't ever be another woman who could, in any way, misinterpret my actions.

For a while I again concentrated solely on work, the finance company was coming on very nicely. I had two garages that gave me all their business, and I got other custom when some of my clients demanded Midland Finance when they bought from other garages. The bakery was earning its keep. We all lived out of it without making any great profits. I was still working about fifteen hours a day, but a great many people in the fifties and early sixties worked almost as long. Dad was still having his annual heart attacks. He was in and out hospital, but in between he seemed to be well enough. I asked the doctor what could be done.

"Nothing really. He's lost weight, but that doesn't seem to have helped much. He seems to be fit enough."

"Fit enough, except that he keeps having heart attacks."

The doctor walked away, he could see I was exasperated.

A lad I knew asked me if I'd like to go out for a drink, and this now became a regular Saturday night outing. They were a group of lads who went to Nottingham every Saturday, just a boozy night out.

This carried on for some time.

I also began my writing career. I would write bits down, at any time really, on odd bits of paper. It wasn't very good at first, but I was learning my trade. I bought an old typewriter, found I wasn't very good on that either, but I was making a start.

At around this time, at one of my deliveries there was a girl who always seemed to be in and out of one of the shops I supplied. She was blonde, very blonde, about the same size and with hair about the same length, as a girl I had last seen lying on a Northamptonshire road. She always spoke, greeted me like a friend. It was a revelation that I could even speak normally to a blonde, and the point was, I hadn't even realized at first the significance of the hair colouration.

Her name was Hazel, she was a housewife with time on her hands, and one day saw me scribbling on a piece of brown paper before I had driven away.

She looked through the van window, "Anything interesting?" she asked.

"Oh, it's just that I am trying to write a book, but at the present rate I'll probably die of old age long before it's done," I said, laughing.

"On bits of brown paper?" Her tone was quizzical.

"I type it out when I've got the time, usually Saturday afternoons or Sundays. Trouble is, I'm not too good on the typewriter either."

"I could type it for you if you like."

"You wouldn't offer if you saw my old machine."

"I don't mind, and I've plenty of time."

"I couldn't afford to pay you, I'm sorry."

"Oh, it's all right, it'll give me something to do."

So Hazel was now my unpaid typist who unravelled my atrocious spelling and never complained.

I saw her husband once or twice. He appeared to be an odd sort of bloke, never wanting to speak, at least not to me. In fact, when I came through the front door to drop some of my scribble at the house, he would instantly get up and walk out of the back door.

I took her round the town on my rounds once or twice, enough to convince me my phobia was gone. I still only had eyes for black-haired girls. Not that there were any.

I was still spending Saturday nights boozing in Nottingham.

Hazel suddenly told me one day, about a year later, that she was going to leave her husband.

"Where are you going?" I asked, more for conversation than anything else.

"I've got a job in Nottingham."

"How will you look after the kids?" I asked, naively.

"I'm leaving them with an aunty, she's going to look after them."

"What about your husband?"

"He'll probably never notice I'm gone, until his dinner isn't on the table, or his clothes aren't washed and ironed."

"Oh."

"You will come to see me, won't you?"

"You know about my Dusky, don't you, what if she suddenly comes back?" Millie had always been paramount in my incessant scribbling.

"I'll have to take that chance."

"I've got a terrible track record."

"You will come?" she repeated.

"I'll come."

"I'll give you a ring, and we will arrange something."

"Look's as if I'll have to take the typewriter away then."

She smiled. "It will be all right, you know."

"I'll come, but remember, it'll only be at weekends, and I cannot, and will not, make any promises."

She gave me an address.

It was on the Saturday the phone rang. "Where are you?"

"I was just thinking of going to Nottingham with the lads."

"Don't tell me you've forgotten you were going to see me?"

"I thought you said you would give me a ring, after you have settled in."

"I'd done that in five minutes."

"I'll come down, meet you in town, in about forty-five minutes."

She named a pub at the corner of Mansfield Road and Parliament Street. It's long gone now, under a big new shopping complex.

Still far from certain, I arrived. I told myself this will probably last no longer than a host of others. I would let her down as gently as possibly. How little I knew.

We ran into my drinking buddies later on. If she was in any way put out with their forthright attitude, she gave no sign. They were always a bit raucous, especially as the night wore on. We stayed with them a while, then they said they were going to a party and we could come as well if we wanted.

"Do you feel like an hour at this party?"

"All right," she replied.

"We don't have to stop long. In fact I don't want to stop anyway, I was working all last night."

We arrived at the house with a crate of ale. There was no one in. The host obviously hadn't been informed that she was having visitors. This was the sort of thing they were inclined to do.

We had stopped and left the bread van in the next street and walked round. I certainly wasn't prepared for the sight that met my eyes. On the top of the roof was Jasper, one of the lads. A window had been left open and he had decided to gain entry that way. The next thing was the sound of a police siren.

Nora, who lived there, came round the corner with her boyfriend. Ralph, another of the lads, shouted for Jasper to jump, he did and suffered a broken ankle. Ralph would say afterwards he hadn't said he would catch him.

Nora let out a startled cry, "Oh God, what are you fools up to now?" as she left the lad she had been with and rushed towards the scene.

Eventually, everyone calmed down and an ambulance which had been called took Jasper off to hospital with a suspected broken ankle. The explanation was that a neighbour had seen someone climbing on the roof, suspected a break-in and phoned the local law.

Now, back in the sixties if the police were called they came. They were not too busy filling out all the forms so as to be unavailable. They were visible and quite ready to tackle most situations. Luckily common sense prevailed in this case and, after questioning all concerned, they left with a bit of a caution and peace returned.

We had left before the hullabaloo began.

One day the lads were in the *Dog* which was a pub along Parliament Street. They had got some books of raffle tickets which they had been trying to sell, without a lot of success. "What's the cause?" I asked.

"Oh," Ralph said, "it's for a trip they are trying to get up for the old folks in Selston, to take them to the seaside."

"Here," I suggested, "give them to me I'll see what I can do."

I sold the three full books to the same people in the pub that they hadn't been able to sell to. I gave them the money, but afterwards I strongly suspected I had been duped. They were just making some money for themselves. I resolved never to be involved in any other scams like that again.

Chapter 5

Now we just paired off with a couple we had just met, Fay and Paul. She seemed to me to think a lot of herself, but Paul was on the fringes of the crazy gang and he was all right. Hazel seemed to like Fay. She went down to her house a bit during the week, when I wasn't available, so it all worked reasonably well.

This carried on for quite a long time, then Fay and Paul decided to get married. We weren't told and weren't invited, that was their business, they could do as they liked. Hazel thought differently and she asked me to take her to the church. I reluctantly agreed, saying we would leave immediately after the ceremony and pointing out they didn't want us there.

I tried to keep to the background but Paul saw me and, as soon as he reasonably could, came over. From his actions it became obvious it had been Fay who hadn't wanted our involvement. He made us welcome and his new bride had no alternative but to join us.

After a while I said, "We should go."

But Paul insisted we stayed. I looked directly at Fay, who now added her voice to the invitation.

I believe we went to the reception, but didn't stay too long We saw little of them after that, I'd no intention of being an unwelcome guest.

Around this time I decided it might be a good idea to teach Hazel to drive and I told her to apply for a driving licence. I'd taught several of my van lads to drive. It was partly selfish as I was often tired from my ridiculously long working periods, and if she could take some of the driving off me when we were out at the weekend, I'd be grateful for that sometimes. She was getting on all right, but with only the weekends it would take a while. So I told her to get some lessons, I'd pay and she would pass a test quicker.

"If you don't pass first time you will have to pay for your own then."

I was making a commitment, even if I didn't see it that way. This was only the second time in my life that I had made a gift. The last time was when I had lost Millie.

Shortly after this my maternal grandmother came to stay with us. She had always seemed so fit and well, but now she became ill. She was in her late eighties and I suppose it was just advancing years. Anyway she became bedfast, so we had a procession of my mother's family who now visited us. Public transport was the normal way of travel in the early sixties, so I felt duty bound to offer to take some of them back home.

I remember when Sis, the eldest of them after my mother, came one weekend and I took her back to Burton-on-Trent. The journey would have been more than two and a half hours by bus. This was pre-mobile phone era, so I had to go via Nottingham to let Hazel know I would be late coming to see her if I could get there at all. To strengthen my case I took Sis up to see her. Sis was less than impressed to have to climb to the top floor of a four-storied Victorian building. Sis suggested Hazel came back to Burton, all three of us in the van, that way she wouldn't be on her own all night. So we all went.

Another of her sisters worked in the bowling alley and Sis wanted to give her a progress report on her mum. So we ended up playing a game of bowls at one of those new bowling alleys that were just starting to appear in the larger towns.

Another week it was one of her brothers who came. He sat alone with his mother in a cold room for something like two hours. As far as I know he wasn't even offered a drink. Mother seemed to have some sort of hostility towards him, so I hadn't met him before. So, even though he also lived in Burton I thought I'd better not offer to take him back. I thought it was because he had been involved in some scandal or other, but I would later find it was to do with him passing to go to university. The whole of the family had to make financial sacrifices to allow him to go. Later other siblings also passed to go, but as all the available money had been lavished on him the younger one's didn't have the opportunity to go. This was accepted, until he had suddenly thrown the lot up to support a girl he had got pregnant, so the sacrifices had been in vain. It was now too late for the others.

Well, as far as I could see, no one else seemed to be put out because of it, and he had married and they had spent the whole of their lives seemingly happily enough. I told Sis that if he came again, I'd certainly take him back.

Sis came often though and we now developed the ritual of picking Hazel up and calling at the bowls hall on the Saturday nights. Sis didn't make the mistake of walking up the stairs again, I had to fetch Hazel.

Sis told my family that I seemed genuinely fond of Hazel and suggested they should invite her over. They had their fingers burnt every time they had tried to 'oil the wheels' and were content to let things take their course.

Sis told Hazel what had transpired and she replied, "I think it's the fact that I am married, and I wouldn't be accepted."

But Sis assured her that she didn't think it was anything to do with this, and they were very worried about the whole way I was living my life.

"Anything that shakes him out of his state of mind." These were the words that my mother had apparently used.

Dad suggested that another woman (Millie) had totally bewitched me.

They had both seen a procession of girls that had come and been abruptly dismissed by me in the previous year or two. They were not keeping their fingers crossed.

If anyone had a reason to complain it was Hazel. There had been occasions when I had come to see her and immediately fallen asleep. So she actually liked the idea of going to Burton, she at least saw me awake.

My grandmother eventually passed away. Now Sis hadn't the reason to come and we didn't go to Burton.

Some little time afterwards I had a visit from the girl who had the breakdown. She had been invited in and was there when I had come off my rounds. I was trying not to upset her in any way, just hoping she'd go. It began as a most formal meeting, and as I recall she drank some tea.

"I realize I shouldn't have sprung it on you at the party."

"No."

"I didn't stay either, you know."

"You would have to, it was your party."

"Well I didn't, I wasn't feeling too well."

"It must have been the only party in history when the host didn't stop. You could have said it had been a joke."

"Everybody knew what I was going to do."

"You should have mentioned it to me."

"You might not have agreed, but I didn't think you would let me down like that."

There was a silence for a while. Neither of us knew what to say. Then in a very quiet voice she said, "Do you really hate me so much?"

"I never hated you."

"I thought you might have come to see me when I was so ill."

"For one thing I didn't see anyone who could have told me that you were ill, and secondly it would have given you the wrong message."

"You do hate me."

"It's not you, it's me that's wrong, and you'll soon find someone who's far better than me."

"I told your mother once that you never make love to me. I asked her if there was some reason."

"I would have liked to have been a fly on the wall at that meeting." I knew my mother's odd attitude to sex outside marriage.

"She didn't answer, I don't think she heard me."

After a silence I said, "I'll take you home."

As I pulled up outside the house her mother was just going in. She asked me if I would come in.

"No, I've just brought her back."

She looked at me as if for an explanation.

"Look, we are not getting back together, she just called for a chat." Then I drove off. I didn't want to be involved in this.

I didn't expect to see her after that, but sure enough, I had a phone call a couple of days later.

"What if I let people know I am pregnant?" she began.

"Well you are not, as far as I know anyway." What the hell was she thinking of?

Now, over the last year there had been perhaps half a dozen girls who could have called that bluff. I had always thought I had been very careful, but if a girl got pregnant in the days before the advent of the pill, in my opinion it was certainly the man's fault.

But this was the one girl who had no pull in that way, I had never touched her. I don't know the reason why, but I hadn't the slightest desire for that sort of contact. She had certainly tried hard enough, God knows she had. Her friends knew she had, perhaps I now knew the reason for my reluctance.

"You aren't answering me," her voice continued. It sounded somehow strange, somehow far away.

"I don't think there is any reason why I should."

I put the receiver down and stood looking at it for a long time. It didn't ring again.

That Saturday night I stayed at Hazel's flat. On the Sunday morning I took her out and we pulled up beside a lake. She was a long way from her home and it would have been difficult for her to get out and say she was walking back.

I told her about the recent events with Margaret.

"Is she pregnant? she asked.

"Of course she isn't, I have never touched her."

"She wouldn't say that if it wasn't true."

"She would say anything, the girl is unstable."

"Why are you telling me this then."

"Because I don't know what she might do next."

"You know, now that I think of it, I don't know what you are up to all week. I only see you at weekends."

"I'm working."

"Why don't you take me home with you to meet your family?"

"All right I will, but I can't guarantee the reception."

So it was that I arrived back home with Hazel.

"Well, I brought her home," I said to my folks, in not too pleasant a way. I thought I was being pressured on all sides. "It's her idea, not mine."

Mum and dad were already eating their dinner.

My mum said, "You had better share his dinner. I'm sorry, I would have prepared you some if I had known you were coming."

We both ate our dinners in silence, I didn't know what to say. As for my family, they couldn't have given her a bigger welcome. In fact, after a while, they spent their time chatting like old friends.

Eventually I suggested I should take her home. "I want a couple of hours sleep, before I start work," I added.

The family seemed reluctant for her to go, and told her she would be welcome at any time.

She looked straight at me. "I'll come any time, maybe he won't want to bring me again."

"Are you twisting my arm again?"

Dad said, "I'll invite you if he doesn't."

I took her back with me the following weekend. Dinner was set for us both this time.

I kept some learner plates on the van so she could drive herself home and I only had to drive back. After a weekend or two of this, mother told her she had made a bed up so that she could stay and catch a bus back in the morning, if she wanted.

We lived in this rambling, early Victorian building attached to the bakery and we had plenty of spare rooms. So she soon got into the habit of stopping overnight. The irony being that, because she stopped overnight, I saw less of her than if I had been going to see her in Nottingham. If I didn't have to get ready to go out on the Saturday I'd invariably find I had some job to do, and she would be left with my parents. Still, she didn't seem too upset about that. Even though it meant she had to get up to catch the bus at seven in the morning for a monotonous, sixteen-mile bus journey, as well as an extra tram trip across town at the other end.

Dad finally suggested she should give up the flat. It would save the money. She was prepared to make that commitment. I only realized afterwards, but I didn't protest too much. Secretly, I suppose I must have liked this loose arrangement.

She would say afterwards that my dad was her pal.

For my part I certainly wasn't seeing any more of this girl who lived just down the corridor.

One day, some months afterwards, she said, so that the family could hear, "My divorce has come through now. If you will not marry me, then I'd better start to find somewhere else to go."

Marriage had never been mentioned. As I had said, I'd got used to this loose arrangement of this girl down the corridor, and I don't think I would have bothered to find another girl. I wasn't even thinking of Millie now, and of course the question was barbed. 'If you want me I'll stay but…'.

"Yes I'll marry you, sometime," I said.

Hazel's attitude was she had waited long enough, her body clock was ticking, and sometime wasn't good enough. The next night she said she had been to the registry office and had made the arrangements, this was going to be it.

"I've seen Pete and Jean (friends who lived near the flat), we will stay overnight at their house. You will be going out with Pete on your stag night. I've invited one or two others, it'll be at the registry office next Saturday, we have got things sorted. And we will spend Saturday night at the *Royal* in London, we can stay as long as we like."

"And who will work on Friday night, and what if I don't want to spend Friday in Nottingham?"

"I've sorted it with dad. We have got someone in to do the night shift, and the round, for a day or two."

"But…"

"No buts, you said you would marry me, now is the time."

"I'll come down on the Saturday."

"No you won't, I know you, it wouldn't happen."

"Can't we just think about this for a little while?"

"It's all arranged. Either you are there, or you will have to jilt me at the registry office, in front of all our friends."

"I wouldn't do that."

"I don't think you would, but I don't want to leave things to chance."

I had the stag night. We got married. It was July 1965, nine years since Millie had gone away.

She said to me, during the actual ceremony, "It's not too late yet, you can still pull out."

I replied, "I agreed didn't I?"

It was during the ceremony that I had another surprise. I learned her maiden name. Perhaps I had heard it before and not noticed. Her initials were HMH. Millie didn't use the first H, but it was the same initials. So that meant every girl I had known since Millie went shared her initials. It didn't make any difference really, but what a coincidence.

The official who performed the wedding ceremony looked as if he had forgotten just what he was supposed to be doing. His face, indeed his whole demeanour, would have been more appropriate had it been a funeral. He certainly wasn't helping my mood. But even so, I was surprised to see the wedding photos. My face, in this sea of happy faces and on every picture, looked as if I had a gun in my back. I wonder how many of the guests would have forecast a long and happy marriage.

We went to London, shared our wedding night, and I managed to even spoil that by insisting I had to be back for work on the Sunday night.

Our wedding had been a disaster, but then the day after we returned it got worse. I had worked as usual and my new bride chose to get the photographs of Millie out of the drawer where they were kept. And as I came into the room she was busy tearing them up and throwing them on to the open fire.

"What the hell are you doing?" I thundered, at the same time trying to grab the pieces out of the flames and burning my hand in the process. At that moment I probably hated this girl more than I had ever hated anyone in my whole life.

The two or three bits I managed to save were no good in isolation so I threw them back in and went outside to cool off. When I returned, Hazel wasn't there.

I asked my parents, "Has she gone yet?"

By the time I had finally calmed down I thought, what has she really done, she destroyed some pictures, but I carry Millie in my heart.

My dad said, "Go and talk to her, she's very upset."

It was on the tip of my tongue to retort, "I am very upset," but I didn't.

We both needed some time to reflect.

She came down a little later on and we quietly sat and ate a meal together. Neither of us could find any words to say. The family tried to help to broach the silence but I went to bed with nothing resolved. It would soon be time to start work. My wife got in beside me a little later, timidly coming in contact with my back.

After a while she said, "I didn't think you would be so upset."

"No."

She held my hand and didn't say anything for a little time.

"We had better get a little sleep," I said.

Later on she would tell me she didn't sleep the whole night.

It was about two weeks later, once more we were in bed together, and I had the strangest feeling starting inside me, something I had completely forgotten.

I told her immediately. "I love you," I said.

I felt her body stiffen under mine.

"I never expected to hear you say those words."

"I never expected to say them."

We began our married life that night, as it should be, two people blissfully unaware of the world around us, and content in our own little world.

It had been about three years since we had met, and we had been married about three weeks before I finally realized the way I felt.

So it was with my wife that I learned the secrets of making love, as opposed to the bob-basics of sex. She would tell me a long time afterwards that that was the first time she really believed our life together was meant to last.

It was about the time of our marriage that the finance company collapsed.

I had £96,600 owing to me at the time and I was still doubling my money every twelve and a half months. I was about three years and five months away from my first million pounds, nothing could possibly go wrong. Then the government in its wisdom decided to alter the rules. Too many of these backstreet car dealers were selling shoddy cars, and before anyone could complain, they were long gone. Henceforth. the finance company would be liable for any necessary repairs.

Both the garages I dealt with had been in business for at least ten years and as far as I know they were supplying decent cars. I had many clients who were on their third or fourth car from the same garage, so they must have been satisfied. Now, if a payment wasn't on time and I was obliged to send a reminder, I would invariably get a standard reply to the effect that, 'Well, I don't think I should pay any more, I have not been satisfied since the start, there is this or that defect.'

I phoned my debt-collector-lawyer. He was obviously well acquainted with the legislation, but somehow hadn't found the time to bring me up to date.

"It's a tricky one," he conceded. "It's new legislation and hasn't been tested in the courts yet."

"What can I do?"

"My advice is nothing, you would need a barrister and they aren't cheap. The best thing is to let someone else test the waters, and just wait."

"And what about all these people who are not paying their instalments?"

"My advice is to let it go, it'll be cheapest in the long run."

I never made the million. In fact, so many got in on the act I only just got enough money back to cover the amount I owed.

Neither of the two garages I dealt with could get anyone to take their finance business and both closed their doors not long afterwards. I really wonder who gained, when the cheap car market collapsed shortly afterwards.

Still, I had my new bride and I lost the company with few regrets. After all, I had never had any money out of it, just the knowledge that the money was there on paper, and that one day I would have been a very rich man.

Now my riches could be counted in the love of my lovely bride, and that was certainly more than I deserved.

Towards the end of the following year I had a daughter as well, I was ecstatic. I was so proud of both my wife and our new family. Even though I still worked all those ridiculous hours, my life now seemed complete.

Dad's final and inevitable heart attack happened in 1968. Because he had these so often and was always all right after a week or two, it was a shock he wasn't going to be around any more. I was devastated. He had taken to pushing our daughter around in her pram, and he still was the man running the firm really.

It seemed he had been determined to hang around at least until he had been sure I was settled. Now he was gone.

"He was my friend too," Hazel said one day.

She thought I was pushing her out of my own personal grief. It was something we had to share, and she intended to be part of it. I had to get through it in my own way. Somehow or other, I did.

I didn't ever remember saying this, but months afterwards Hazel told me I had said, at some time after own daughter Samantha was born, "I just need a son now, and my whole world will be complete." If I did, it was almost a disaster.

It was a few years later that she presented me with our son.

I went and registered the birth and I named him William after my dad.

Hazel said, "You didn't mean me to have any say in that did you?" Still, she liked it anyway. I remember all the talk about names when our girl was born, we couldn't think of a name between us.

It was the day I had gone to the hospital and got acquainted with my new family that a doctor called me into the office.

"What the hell do you think you were doing?"

"What do you mean, what am I supposed to have done?" I asked, totally perplexed.

"The warning was plain enough, another child could have killed her."

"Is she all right?" I was badly shaken.

"She is, but you might not have been so lucky."

"I didn't know."

"But she knew, and she said you wanted a son."

"More than anything in this world, I want my wife," I told him.

"I have to ask you for your permission to make sure this doesn't happen again."

"Of course," I replied. "Anything, but what does she say?"

"She say's it's up to you."

"What did you think you were doing?" I asked her.

"I just knew it would be all right."

"I can't manage without you, you do know that, don't you?"

"You told me you wanted a son."

"Maybe I did, but not at any cost."

This incident was very sobering for me, and reinforced my feeling that I had a very special wife. One thing was now certain, I could never let her down, ever. I thought of the girls I had known and came to the conclusion that, with one single exception, all the lot of them had probably been far too good for me.

Life carried on much as before, I was still maintaining my normal work pattern.

Two years after my dad's death, and in the year our son had been born, I had the letter from the tax office. I had to pay death duties on dad's estate. I had the figure and it seemed more money than I had ever seen in my life. (I never actually saw any money from the finance company.) I went to see my accountant.

"What am I supposed to do with this?"

He looked at it.

"I didn't expect it would be anywhere near as high as that," he said.

"Can I appeal, it's got to be a mistake?"

"No, it'll have to be paid, somehow."

The accountant suggested the bank, so I saw the bank manager.

"I wouldn't lend you a penny on that business," he said.

"Well what will happen now?"

"Oh, they will sell the place up."

"Where can I go, I haven't any money?"

"Best thing you can do is to put your name down for a council house and hope you have some friends on the council. Otherwise you will be out on the street."

I decided to see the tax inspector. I arrived with the last year or two's accounts, but he never even looked at them.

"What can I do?" I asked him. "You can see the figures, I'll not be able to raise that sort of money in a lifetime. You might as well ask for a million and be done with it." I told him of my visit to the bank manager, and what he had said. I also told him about my wife and new baby. "We can't go and live in a tent," I added.

He just smiled. "Don't worry, it won't come to that. All we ask is that you make some reasonable attempt to pay."

"How?" I asked.

"Look, just leave it two years, then we will meet again. In the meantime, just you look after that wife and that baby."

"Yes but that will only defer it. I will still have to pay all this money, and frankly, I don't see how I can ever get enough money to pay it."

"In two years time we will talk about what you can pay, and no one will dispossess you, that much I will promise. You will have to pay no more than you reasonably can."

I left with a friendly handshake. Then as I got to the door I stopped. "What if another tax inspector is here, he might have different ideas?"

"I will leave notes and anyone else will read them." I still stood half in and half out of the door when he added, "Don't worry about anything, it'll all be all right."

I related all this to my accountant a few days later.

"You must have made some impression on him, I wouldn't have dared to even try that."

"I hadn't any option."

I made light of things to Hazel, oozing a confidence I was far from feeling. "We are going to be all right. I will have to find something for the death duties in about two years time, they don't know how much yet."

I had kept the original figure from her. It wasn't my normal practice, but having the baby and all that, I hadn't wanted to worry her. Now I had to try to find some way of generating more money. Events like this sharpen the focus.

I remembered one of dad's sayings, 'Remember you will never fail, until the day you stop trying to succeed'.

I started looking around to see what opportunities were presented.

They were building a huge new shopping and market complex in the nearby town of Sutton-in-Ashfield. It was time I found out just what was happening. After wandering around totally unchallenged amidst the signs of organized chaos, I came across a building I would later discover to be the new market hall. I started to talk to a carpenter who was finishing work in one of the shops.

"Are each of the shops already allocated?" I asked.

"Don't know mate," came back the answer, "better ask him."

He indicated a man who looked like an old collier who had just infiltrated the place. He appeared to be 'rubber-necking' the same as I was. I walked over and repeated my enquiry to him.

"Yes, they have all been spoken for, since the project was set up."

"Oh."

"Yes," he repeated. "I was the first to bring up the idea at the council meeting years ago."

"I didn't know about it, don't get into Sutton a lot."

"What is your line of business?"

"I'm a baker."

He took me across to a double stall.

"This is the place earmarked for the bread and cake shop." He was obviously proud of his achievements.

"And you say it's already gone?" I said.

"Sorry, it's a baker from Nottingham, he was about the first to put his name down, way back when the plans had only just been drawn up."

"And will there be a chance of another stall?"

"No, we want to be fair, just one of each trade, as much as we can."

"It's a pity."

I was thinking, there were disadvantages in always being at work, you just don't know what is happening under your own nose.

The councillor offered a lifeline.

"You can put your name down, in case of any cancellations. I don't hold out a lot of hope though."

I filled in the form.

"How much is the rent?"

"It's going to be twenty-three pounds a week."

I was surprised, but I gave no indication. The rent for a house was only about a fiver a week. I'd have taken it anyway, I was in a 'muck or nettles' situation. It was all too recent, the prospects of the bakery being sold and living with my family in a tent.

Well, there might be other opportunities somewhere, but it was unlikely that I'd find anywhere as convenient as this.

I didn't mention to my wife where I had been, no point anyway, nothing would come of it. For now I had the unique chance to get acquainted with my new son. And of course, some sleep as it would soon be time to start work.

It was about three weeks afterwards when the phone call came.

Would I like to go and see the councillor?

The shop girl had answered the phone, written it down and passed the slip of paper to Hazel. I was still out on my rounds.

"I thought you said they had said we weren't going to be thrown out?" she accused me later on when I came in.

"We're not, at least I don't think we are. The taxman promised I didn't even have to go and see him for another two years."

"Why have you put your name down for a council house then?"

I was thoroughly bewildered.

She passed me the message that the shop assistant had written down: Councillor Gregory wondered if you would like to go down to see him.

I read it uncomprehendingly for an instant, then the name suddenly registered. It was the man from the market hall at Sutton. I smiled.

"This is another kind of council house, and yes I would love to go and see the councillor."

Hazel was holding our baby, unable to understand my sudden hilarity.

I fished inside my smock pocket, found a number and rang it.

"No, I am not doing anything particular at the moment, I'll come straight away."

"No, I'll come straight away," Hazel mocked. "If I want you to do something it's, sorry I have to get some sleep. Now some councillor rings and it's drop everything and go."

"Oh sweetheart, this might not be anything, or it could be the answer to all our prayers." She looked at me and I went over and gave her a kiss. "Whatever happens, I promise to give you a blow by blow explanation as soon as I get back, trust me."

The bread van was on its way to Sutton.

What it turned out to be was that the Nottingham bread man had been to see the stall. He thought it was too big and suggested it be cut down to half size and half rent.

"What do you think of that?" Mr Gregory asked me.

"Well," I said, "I'll take the other half, or if you prefer it, I'll take the lot."

"I thought you might say that. What I shall do is to bring it up at the next council meeting. I will report all that's happened, and I'll say you are my first choice now and it will go to the vote."

"Has this Nottingham baker man got a lot of friends on the council?"

"We will find that out at the meeting. In the meantime my secretary will write and tell him that others are interested, and it will be discussed at the next meeting."

I went over and shook his hand. "I am grateful for what you are doing for me."

"I'm just doing what I believe will be the best for the council."

Hazel was sitting waiting for an explanation. I explained about the new development, and the inclusion of the market hall. "It could be just what we need," I added. Then I mentioned the rent.

"We haven't the money to splash out on something like that," was her immediate reaction.

"Look at it this way. The place is fully-furbished, there is nothing to do but to take our stuff down there. There is no way we will ever be able to pay the death duties unless we can generate some more money. All the cash will be retail, we won't have to give anyone 20%. We won't need a man and a van running around all day, and with a bit of luck we won't have so much waste. And because it's a brand new project, people will go to see just what is there. Hopefully it'll take more money. The council wouldn't fork our millions to create the precinct if they expected no one to use it."

"But we haven't got it yet."

"Perhaps we won't get it, but at least we will have tried. And we can still look out for other projects."

I was suddenly so very tired and I went to bed, it was nearly getting up time.

We had our market. It was 1971. A driver left and another was banned from driving. I wrote personal letters to all the customers they delivered to. I said we wouldn't be able to supply them because the drivers had gone. Everyone thought I was completely off my rocker. But we hadn't made any money, just covered costs, for so long now. I had tried all I knew to generate more sales, without a lot of success. It was going to be 'muck or nettles' now.

I increased the prices of all our cakes. We made exactly the same amount that we would have done from the two vans. We didn't give anyone the 20% and we sold completely out of every crumb.

The following week we increased our sales. We took more money on that market than we had previously on the four vans put together, and we had less money to pay out. Suddenly we were making a healthy profit, and I gave up the other two vans.

Oh, and long before I was due to see the tax inspector again I personally took him a cheque. I shook his hand and thanked him sincerely. I'd paid up the death duties in full. I didn't owe any man a penny.

There was no reasonable excuse for working the night shift any more. Hazel was putting some pressure on me to get someone to do the job. Then, I seemed to have all the time in the world, and nothing to occupy my time. I began my writing again and I joined the Writers Guild. They seemed to believe I had some talents, but I didn't get anything published, other than a short article in a magazine. In the next few years I had written four, 400-page novels, which remain unpublished to this day. I enjoyed it though, and it's always better to have had a go.

Next I started to play golf. Hazel bought me some clubs and arranged for me to play against a couple of chaps I knew. I soon got the bug, though for a time I was hopeless.

The following season I played regularly four or five times a week, and by the end of the year I was playing to about a fourteen handicap.

I remember playing once against a professional golfer. I could out-hit him by a distance, but I wasted a ton of shots around the green. He won it comfortably enough.

Years later, when I started playing a few rounds with my son, I found I had lost this ability to hit the ball for long distances. I didn't know how I'd managed to do it in the first place, or why I couldn't manage to repeat it years later. Age cannot ever understand its inability to challenge youth.

I went into another new indoor market venture, and in 1974 began my new indoor bread shop. It cost me £68,000, including machinery, alterations, shop fittings and repainting, to get the shop and fit it out. I can assure anyone that that was a lot of money in those days but I paid for it over six months. I opened another shop in a converted church, even had a celebrity to open it. I had done all that in a mere four years. I still owed no man a penny, not the bank, and especially not the tax inspector. Nothing could stop me now.

Then I began to play squash, with the same intensity I did everything else. I was forty-three when I first picked up a racket. I remember seeing my doctor at the courts one day and he said, "If I had known you were thinking of doing that, I would have forbidden it."

"Why?" I asked

"The way you always do things, I would have thought you were too old to start."

I laughed.

The friends we stopped with at the time of our wedding had emigrated to Australia just afterwards. They used to phone us from time to time. Hazel was talking to them one day and she turned to me and said, "Pete wants to know when we are coming to see them."

Tell him, "We'll come just after Christmas."

She put the phone down and said, "Do you really mean it?"

We went to Australia at the time when even the most adventurous of the working class families in our area hadn't ventured any further than the Spanish Costas.

Not only Australia, but we also toured South-East Asia as well. The sky was the limit now.

All our vehicles and machinery were brand new. I remember going into a filling station where there was a new car and a new van standing in the showroom. Hazel was with me and she was looking at the Mini. "Nice isn't it?" she said.

"Do you want it I asked?"

She turned her face towards me, smiled and said, "Can we afford that as well?"

"Why not?"

Most petrol stations at that time filled the petrol tank for you. The man took the money and went to get you the change. He was returning with our change now and I said, "I'll have the Mini."

He looked as if he thought I was joking. But I convinced him and he fetched the owner. I came away from that petrol station having bought the van as well. I wrote the cheque there and then.

I was playing squash most nights, in the Derbyshire league, the Notts. League, and in all the internal club leagues as well.

Then I decided to buy a house in Florida. A new build, complete with swimming pool and grounds. All paid for, and included in the books so the taxes were paid in full, as I went along.

I was happy. I had a lovely wife. She had given me my two wonderful kids. I had money for everything I could possibly want.

We toured the world again, took in the southern hemisphere and the Pacific, and we toured America. We were so very happy.

Nothing could go wrong. This was different to the finance company, this time I had money to spend. It wasn't something on the books owing to me that would come eventually. This was real.

Chapter 6

I t did go wrong. I can tell you the day, the very minute it went wrong. It was my fault. I gave it all away.

We were at our house in Florida. During that morning I went out with John, a big London developer, and Steven who was involved with the property people. The talk had been of fishing. I said I couldn't see anything more boring than sitting for hours by a cold, cheerless English river and then at the end of the day, cold and miserable, having to throw all you had caught back into the water, always assuming you had caught anything. Then you went home to try to get the circulation back into your limbs.

John had immediately offered to take me marlin fishing on his yacht, in the Gulf of Mexico. Steven countered by saying he would take me up into the Arctic in his private jet. The idea being you cut a hole in the ice, fish were attracted by the light and you could pull the fish out continuously until you were just too tired to carry on. You then cooked and ate the fish while still on the ice. Nothing could be nicer than fresh fish cooked where you had pulled them from the icy waters. Of the two I certainly would have preferred the marlin, I think.

We had looked around a whole catalogue of different properties and John had ended up buying half a dozen different places. They would be an investment. Now there was a man who was seriously rich.

Then I had gone back to our home, it was a glorious day. The warm sun of the near tropics shone from an unbroken clear blue sky. It was an idyllic scene with Hazel and the kids already splashing in the pool. "What have you been buying now?" she asked

"Nothing. John has though, he's bought a whole heap of properties."

She smiled at me. We had everything we really wanted and we were gloriously content. The business was almost running itself. I was always surprised when we returned from these holidays that the money seemed to increase more when I wasn't there.

"One day maybe, but it's too soon for me to think of anything else yet," I mused, still thinking of John's investments.

I slipped out of my clothes and into that cool water beside my family. I was surely the luckiest man in the whole world.

Hazel and the kids got out a little later, saying they had been in long enough. I swam up and down for a while longer, then having got out, partially dried myself before letting the sun's rays finish the work.

There was the slightest of breezes. I was sitting on a deckchair, my mind wandering to the way my life had gone. I thought of Millie, of how I had been so afraid to tell her that poverty was all I had to offer. She would have loved this. How long ago was that? I began to calculate. Could it really have been twenty-one years? Now I had all this. I had the most wonderful wife that I scarcely deserved, and my two kids, that made my life fulfilled.

Still the mind was tormenting me. Where was my Dusky now?

I had all the money I could ever spend in a lifetime. I didn't really need all this. I thought, I would willingly give it to that brown-skinned beauty. Then I had the strangest feeling come over me, as though I had actually given her the money. I remembered I had the same feeling once before, when I had drawn every penny out of my building society account and given it to the woman I loved.

Hazel had changed now and was standing close to me. When she spoke it was as if she had read my mind.

"You were thinking about her," she accused.

Neither of us had mentioned Millie for years. Why had she said that? I felt strangely moved.

"That was a funny thing to say."

"Maybe it was, but I know." I didn't answer, so she continued, "Would you still leave me if she came back?"

"Of course not, I have the best wife in the world, and I love my kids."

"What if you find a dolly bird?"

"Especially not, I wouldn't leave you for all the dolly birds in the world. Now enough of this daft talk. Let's go out and get a meal." I wanted to change the subject.

That weekend our holiday was over and we went back to Blighty. I was driving back home from the airport, passing our hot bread shop and saw they were painting double white lines in the middle of the road in front of the property. This was the latest innovation of fiddling public servants. It was new and I didn't even know the significance.

I would learn it meant 'no parking', and we relied principally on passing trade. Well there was a wide piece of pavement but when I tried to let customers leave their cars there whilst they were in the shop, I was told in no uncertain terms by the local police, "You can't do that."

Then, to make things worse, there was a policeman who lived just round the back of the place who now seemed to be making it his personal project to put a parking ticket on every vehicle that stopped. What had I ever done to upset them?

Inside the shop the walls, which had been lined with plasterboard by the previous owner, had now started to bend and warp with the heat of the bakery. It was beginning to look a mess. It needed some tender loving care. I would have to see what could be done.

Worse, I was to find out we seemed to have an infestation of everything imaginable. I phoned the council and told them we seemed to have mice. They sent their pest control officer and I found out we had ants as well. This must have been because of the buckled walls. I'd have to put ant killer all over the place. After discussing this for a while, I decided to go to Sutton and look at what was happening at the unit inside the converted church. Outside, a man with one of those sandwich-boards was walking up and down. He was proclaiming that this was a house of God and it had been desecrated by commercial activities. He was loudly berating any who entered.

Now, in the seventies people still at least paid lip service to religion. I went inside to be told by my shop assistant, "Oh I'm glad you have come, I don't know what to do, people just won't come past him. Everyone's sales have taken a nosedive. It's not just us, and it's not my fault," she added, piteously.

"No I can see that," I said.

Nevertheless, when the lease came up for renewal a few weeks afterwards I didn't renew it.

I'd go next to the indoor market. I was in need of some cheering up.

Now, over the last few months a string of shops all round the market had started selling hot bread baked on the premises. Even though this included a big supermarket, which was just adjacent, it hadn't made one iota of difference to our sales. Now one final hot bread shop was on the verge of opening. This was just in the doorway to the market. I'd known all about this, but I hadn't given it a moment's thought. All the others were already plying their wares, but our sales hadn't suffered one little bit.

Now, however, everyone entering the market had to pass this new place. They would have about six girls serving on the counter and, what's more, they were giving people vouchers to get free bread, cobs or cakes. To these people money wasn't an issue, they just wanted the trade. When this place opened I would lose about £800 per week from my takings.

Customers kept telling us they wouldn't buy from the new place, however. They had these free vouchers but they would just spend them and afterwards they would be returning to us. But in spite of all assurances our trade was very down.

I tried the market at Alfreton. I was fully expecting it would be burnt down, or some other disaster. Takings were down a little, but nothing to add to my uneasiness.

When the dust settled, I was £2,200 per week down. Approximately 40% of my business was gone in an instant but all my expenses were the same.

Now, suddenly, I didn't have the money to do up the hot bread shop. It was difficult to see how I could reduce my expenses. Money was flying out and not coming back. I was in trouble.

I discussed this with Hazel and she said, "I thought we were spending too much."

I made her see that that hadn't been the case. I had never owed anything, taxes had always been paid and I had always had money in the bank. Even the house in America had been paid for in cash and fully declared in the books, so there could be no later shocks from the tax man.

Now, frankly, I was broke, or soon would be, unless I could do something soon.

I phoned Steven, the estate manager in America. They had always told me if I wanted to let the house for the holiday market they could guarantee an 80% letting, making me a good income. Any money would be welcome so I told him to go ahead. It would mean that we couldn't go at the drop of a hat, but it didn't look as if we would be going so much anyway. Well, the dollar suddenly went up about 25% against other currencies and no one could afford to go to America any more. In the next three years the property was occupied for just three weeks.

I still had to pay pool maintenance costs. A well known actor, who was a neighbour, had been fined for allowing algae to get on his pool, so it had to be done. Then there were all sorts of miscellaneous expenses including, I remember, a new post box. Someone backed into the old one and smashed it.

I thought of what had happened on that day when the warm rays of the afternoon sun had been drying my body. I wondered if Millie had suddenly obtained a fortune. I hadn't much time to think of her though, I was doing all I could do to ward off an impending collapse.

I eventually lost the hot bread shop. Afterwards I couldn't believe my eyes when I saw workmen painting out those double white lines in the middle of the road. And still later, when the new occupant had painted parking lines on the middle of the wide pavement

In the finish we lost both the cars. If we went out, we were back to the bread van. The American dream and the hot bread shop had gone and I was back working all the hours that came. Not quite so many as I once had to, but a lot. Still, I had my wife and I had my two kids and so I counted myself the luckiest of men.

Hazel had seen the hours I had worked most of my life, so when our daughter took a course in bookkeeping a few years later on she did all she could to discourage her from joining us at the bakery. I didn't know anything about this until much later on. My son, when his time came to find some rewarding occupation, approached me, otherwise he would have been similarly discouraged.

I had always wanted both my kids around me.

I was broke, but the death throes would last for many years yet. I even said to my wife, "If you want a divorce, I wouldn't blame you."

"Why, do you want someone else?"

Why did she always assume that?

"There is never going to be anyone else, there never has been and I am not going to start now. You should know that, but I have let you down so badly."

"You hadn't got anything when I married you. Just because things have gone wrong now, it doesn't make any difference to us."

"It was all my fault, I gave it all away."

"I love you and I always will, so stop this daft talk."

"I love you too, so very much," I replied. I was totally convinced that I had got the best of this bargain.

It was about this time when an American publisher was talking about publishing my latest book. He told me of the American system of putting novels in libraries. I would get a fee every time someone took it out. To ensure that I was known, I would go to New York and appear on a television show. Then there would be the book signing sessions. This would give me some free advertising. Later on I would get the opportunity to go on the network in other cities.

I also went to Nottingham radio station. It was a new initiative to encourage local talent. We split into groups of three and then wrote a short play between us. I wouldn't have thought this format could work, but being involved, I could see the advantage.

Afterwards I told them about my book in America and they said, "When it comes out we will plug it for all its worth."

Eventually the Americans quietly dropped the book, mainly I think, because I suddenly couldn't afford to spend the time in America to be on the television there and for the book signings. It would be very time consuming to pursue my American dream. I was fighting for my bakery life, and just dare not go for a month or two. I had tried to defer it for a while, and they seemed to cool off.

I was still playing squash for various teams, even though I was approaching sixty. I had developed asthma a long time before this and I used an inhaler. Even so, it didn't bother me too much. I was surprised to find just how many outwardly fit squash players used one. Then one day I injured an ankle, a stab of pain through my heel. I visited the medics.

"I'll need some pain killers, there are some very important matches coming up."

The doctor looked at me as if I was barking mad. I was within a few weeks of my sixtieth birthday, when most people just tottered to the local pub, and I wanted pain-killers so that I could run around like a twenty-year-old playing a game as energetic as squash.

"You'll not be able to run around on that for at least six months. I don't think you will be able to play any games like that ever again."

I laughed at that, but agreed to give it a couple of week's complete rest, before coming to see him again.

I never went on a squash court again.

In 1991 I had a heart attack and I was stuck in hospital. I didn't think it was a particularly bad one and I was desperate to get back to work, but they insisted on keeping me in the hospital for a week. When I eventually got back home I couldn't believe the weakness I felt, but I was determined to get back to work as soon as I could.

Two years after that I collapsed with a stroke. I was lying on the floor but the doctor wouldn't come. He said there was nothing that could be done for strokes anyway (nowadays they seem to be a priority). I had to get there to see him. I did get there somehow, but he simply reiterated nothing could be done. The medical opinion is different nowadays. I had lost the power of speech, my right side was useless and the whole of my face was lopsided.

If he would do nothing I would find someone else who might help. I went to a top acupuncturist who I knew. I had to endure a trip up to West Yorkshire, about seventy miles away. He stuck four needles in the top of my head.

"This is all the Chinese do for strokes. There is no point in coming again, it's a one-off treatment. Usually it works, occasionally it doesn't."

It worked and each week I got a little better, either my speech, my face, or my side, gradually I became right. It seemed to take a long time though.

When I eventually saw my doctor he expressed surprise. "I didn't think you would ever get over that."

"Thanks." But it was the acupuncturist, and no thanks to him.

Chapter 7

It was October and the year was 1994 or 1995 and I had been out somewhere with my wife. I was feeling content with life in general, no real problems to shatter the equilibrium. Walking into the house I wasn't thinking of anything in particular. Then I let out a gasp, Millie was standing there. I said, "What are you doing here?"

Hazel said, "What's the matter?"

I looked back at her, and when I looked again Millie was gone. I sat down, I had seen her, of that I was certain. Now, I didn't hide anything from my wife and I wasn't going to start now. I told her exactly what I had seen and she was surprisingly sympathetic.

I believed that, at that very moment, something had happened to Millie. If it was possible, I had to know. I didn't see her again but I sensed that she was around, and always in the same direction. I even got a map out and calculated the direction from the position of the North Star. I was astonished to find it was the direction of the village in which she had once lived.

Now I began to lose weight. I lost four stone in just four months. Hazel was urging me to go to the doctor and eventually even I could see this was a necessity. The doctor examined me and pronounced nothing was physically wrong.

In the meantime I wandered around Millie's old village, and obviously found nothing. What I expected I didn't really know. I even walked around the local cemetery. I must be losing it.

The next time I sensed she was around I asked, "Where can I find you?"

Into my head, immediately, came the reply, "The cherry tree."

What was it, where was it? I had to find out. Again I made my way to the village.

I asked on the street, "Is there a place around here called the *Cherry Tree*, a nursing home or something, anything?"

No one seemed to have heard of it, then someone said. "There's a pub called the *Cherry Tree*."

I had to go back later when the place was open. It turned out to be run-down establishment probably on its last legs. Her name meant nothing to the landlord, but women alter their names, get married. And don't forget, I wasn't looking for this raving beauty I was looking for a woman in her sixties.

I went home disappointed

Then I thought of an idea. The next time I thought about her, I asked about the *Cherry Tree*. When should I go? Into my mind came the time, 'seven o'clock Thursday'.

This was an awkward time for me but I was there. The place was completely empty apart from one man sitting on his own. Another wild goose chase. The man was looking at a glass that was almost empty. More for something to say I nodded at the glass. "Do you want another?"

I bought him one, then he started talking about the old lido clubroom, "It's been closed for thirty-five years." he stated.

I didn't know, didn't really want to talk, so I finished my drink.

"I'd better go," I said.

When I got home I thought, what an odd thing, to talk about a place that had been closed for all that time, and to a complete stranger. Then it struck me, had be really been a stranger, could it have been Al? I hadn't even looked closely at him, hadn't really any idea of how old he might be. I went back the next night but he wasn't there. I told the landlord I had been there the previous night talking to a man. We were the only two people in the pub and did he know who he was.

"No idea mate."

I mentioned Al's name, did it mean anything?

"Not really."

Hazel was getting a bit fed up with my chasing rainbows. Even I was thinking it was hopeless anyway. I'd done all I could. She at least hadn't drawn the connection between the weight loss and what she called my obsession.

I wasn't sensing she was around so much now, and I thought my original idea was probably correct. Something had happened to her.

Then I found out about spiritual churches and I went along. People talked to me about all sorts of things, except the one thing I wanted to know. One speaker told me I would be in the middle of a road accident. He said there would be smashes all round me, I would be in the middle but I would be all right. I had a soldier boy dressed in a red uniform who had put his cloak round me. I would be safe. Oh, and he had been killed, not in the war, but in a minor skirmish. He had been a relative.

Now I had traced my family tree back to the sixteen hundreds and I knew of no family member who had been killed in any conflict. I decided this was totally ridiculous. Just a total waste of time.

My aunty Sis came to see us a while afterwards and I was laughing about this. She said, "But there was a soldier." He had been a cousin of hers. "When I was a kid he visited us, he was my hero, so handsome in a red dress uniform. When I asked later on what had happened to him, I was told he had been killed in a skirmish."

I felt suddenly cold, as if the proverbial man had walked over my grave.

I'd almost forgotten this strange incident when a few weeks afterwards I was driving along the A38 Alfreton bypass. It was an area prone to thick fog banks, more so then than now (the Clean Air Act reduced the pollution), and there was a smash, a great pile up of vehicles. I stopped well short of the carnage, possibly because people had got out of their vehicles and run back along the road waving anything they could to stop the traffic. A hundred yards behind me a further smash happened, but it was the one in front that had been the worst. I would later learn a young woman had been killed.

I didn't think about it until some time later, but I suddenly had cause to feel grateful to my unknown soldier benefactor.

I started to go once more to the spiritualist church. The only other thing they told me was about a fob watch. Apparently this had belonged to my great-grandfather and had been passed down and my dad had it at one time. "This is still in the family," I was told, "get it at all costs."

A different speaker gave me the same message some weeks afterwards. It was all very odd.

I asked my mother about the watch. She had a vague recollection of a watch, but no idea what had happened to it. I asked the only members of my dad's family I was in contact with, and who might have some ideas, carefully making no mention of where I had got my information from, they would probably think I was crackers, but I drew a blank.

I carried on going to the spiritual church for a little while longer, but none of the other speakers seemed to want to talk to me, so I stopped going.

We were comfortable again, nothing like the money we once had, but did it matter? Pete and Jean, our friends in Australia, had both died so we decided to go to New Zealand. A lad who had worked for us years before had emigrated and we had always kept in touch. He'd asked us to go often enough, so we had six weeks over there. It was great time and Roger took us all round the North Island. We saw the sights, generally relaxed, and enjoyed it all.

It was several years after this, towards the end of 2006 when Hazel started to lose weight. Well, I had lost four stone in as many months a few years before, so we weren't alerted to any danger. Eventually she did see the medics and it was panic stations and tests at the hospital. She had the dreaded cancer and we had to go to see the specialists.

The prognosis wasn't good. She would have to go into hospital for more tests. Nothing seemed to be working. I was assured that the specialists were only at the end of the phone, anything I wanted to discus they would willingly talk about. In the meantime, Hazel just got weaker. She had no appetite and they put a thing in her neck to feed her, but still she had no strength, even to sit up unaided. She could hardly stand even with help, to get out of bed to the seat alongside.

I got hold of the specialist's secretary and I asked to see him, but it was a young girl doctor who came to see me. She was a drab looking thing. I remember she had a low cut dress. This was not the time, or the place. Didn't she know this was my wife, she was very ill? The girl looked disgusting, or it could have been that I was so very sensitive at that time.

I asked her where was this specialist who was available any time, day or night.

"I am in charge of this case," she said, not unkindly. "He wouldn't be able to tell you anything that I can't."

I refrained from saying anything that might antagonize her.

"We keep hearing of all these new drugs," I began. "Can't any of them help, I'll pay for anything?"

It was Hazel herself who asked the dreaded question. "How long have I got left?"

"Well, it's incurable," she said.

"How long?" Hazel repeated.

"About nine months," the girl said.

I opened my mouth to say something. Words failed me.

Throughout, Hazel was calm and serene. She'd had had all the treatments. None had worked. She was prepared, I wasn't.

They made me up a bed beside hers in the hospital. It all seemed totally unreal. I lay in the bed beside her, holding her hand, listening to the rhythmic sound of her breathing. Suddenly it stopped. Her hand wasn't cold, or anything like that, but she wasn't breathing. I was out of bed ringing the bell and a nurse came.

"She's gone." Her words barely registered on my numbed brain. I just stood there, probably looking as pathetic as I felt. "Surely you expected it, they must have told you."

"In nine months, that bloody doctor girl said."

"I'll sit with you and hold your hand." The nurse girl was obviously well meaning.

"It's the last thing I need just now. Please, just leave me alone."

She went, saying, "Stay as long as you want." Then as an afterthought, "Have you let anyone know, is someone coming for you?"

I phoned home, then went and sat with her. Nothing seemed real. Hazel was never ill, it was always me. I had the heart attack, I had the stroke, I had asthma, I even sat in the middle of a pile-up in the fog when a woman had died and was unscathed. (Had a soldier really protected me?)

Hazel died within about a month of being told she had nine months. I don't know if she had the best treatment in the world, or if she was just another statistic. I was completely empty. The world was suddenly a different place. People fight for years with the dreaded cancer. It was as if she had given up. Hazel didn't just give up, ever.

Why hadn't it been me? The world was a worse place without her, I wouldn't have mattered.

I remembered she had wanted to go to New Zealand again. We would have been there now. I had said, "Not this year. Let's just go for a few little holidays, next year we can think about it."

I would later find out she had begun getting some New Zealand dollars. I didn't know then. I'd always done things my way. Would this still have happened? Would the hospitals over there have been any better. Would... would...

My son had arrived to take me home.

"Would I be all right on my own?"

What a daft question. People tried to say the right thing. I was not ready for people saying 'the right thing'. I don't think I'll ever be ready. I was empty. It's like nothing else. We were together for forty-two years.

I was lucky in one sense. I still had the bakery, where there were still everyday people that I had to talk to. They had their own lives to lead, paying no more than lip service to anyone else's feelings, and it was better that way.

You get over it, but it doesn't go away... ever.

We scattered the ashes at the crematorium and I picked what I believed to be a flowering cherry. We went several times and the heart shape we had made showed no sign of fading. It seemed the only one where the ashes stayed as they had been put. I told myself it was because she was so special. Then one day I went and the cherry-pink blossom was gone. I was one of those who got the wrong tree, it now had the tell-tale russet red leaves of the copper beech. We even had to go and get a map from the office to verify which was the right tree. How could I have got to the wrong tree? I was pathetic.

About two months afterwards a woman, some thirty years younger than me and with whom I had often had a bit of banter, suggested that we could now go for a few days on holiday together. I was disgusted.

"Nothing can replace my girl, It'll be a long time before I want any other woman."

I have never spoken to her since.

My son and grandson took me to Rome for a three-day sightseeing trip and I succeeded in rupturing my Achilles' tendon. Still, I managed to hobble around, and on return to the local hospital was told just what was wrong. So I had to walk around in a 'Beckham boot' for the next ten weeks. It meant going to the 'Crem' was out. I did try once, but a long walk across uneven grass with one club leg which is longer than the other, and in a wind, is not to be recommended.

Well, I shall soon lose my club leg and regain my independence. It's now about the anniversary of the scattering, so we should be back to the pink flowers.

My daughter has started taking me to the spiritual church again, complete with club foot. Only once have they said anything significant. The conversation went something like this:

She was here, said she was all right, and had told me to watch out for an injury to my right knee and my left ankle. I did hurt my knee, but the ankle turned out to be the right Achilles' heel.

She had also pointed out that the time had come to start my writing career again, this time I might be surprised. It had been a good few years since my unsuccessful novels.

She also said something else, which my daughter didn't pick up on, something which shocked me more than I cared to say. There had always been three people in our marriage.

In the forty-two years of our marriage, plus about three before we actually wed, there had never been any desire for another woman. I didn't take drugs, I didn't drink more than occasionally, I was a total bore.

Was I lying to myself? There had always been a memory, more than that, an obsession with Millie. So much so that it had altered my life. But it's fifty–one years since I saw her. Even if she is still around, she isn't twenty-five any more, she will be seventy-seven now, and I never saw a seventy-seven-year-old with head-turning beauty. Surely my girl couldn't have really feared her still.

I was taking this too literally, but the ankle, the writing, the whole lot had been too close to ignore. I thought of the soldier boy and the other accident from so long ago that had been foretold by a medium. None of this can be real, or can it?

Then there was the fob watch. Two different people had mentioned that, and there did appear to have been a watch, even if I hadn't yet located just what had happened to it.

I'd been a lot of other weeks when whatever messages I had hadn't borne a shred of sense.

A long time ago, when I thought I had seen Millie, no one mentioned anything about it, even though I had gone to the church for a long spell, specifically to find the answer to that one single question.

One other strange thing happened. I had gone to fetch something or other from a local supermarket one day. A lady of about my own age spoke to me. She said, "Do you remember me?"

I looked at her. Something about her seemed a little familiar.

"I think I should."

She told me her name. It was a girl I had known more than sixty years ago, way back in the mist of time. She was the first girl I had ever liked. It was being reminded of her initials that astonished me, MH.

The coincidence was astonishing.

The bakery continues serenely, going from strength to strength, without a great input from me.

It is a new generation with new ideas. The same activity with the bread and cakes, but we make photo cakes now. And another new innovation, under a new company heading 'Eat your photo' we send the pictures all over the country. Some even go to different parts of the world.

I wonder what some of the earlier bakery owners would have made of that? Come to think of it, I bet that dad would have embraced the technology. He was always in the forefront of any innovations.